QUAEEIN

A History and Explorer's Guide

TABLE OF CONTENTS

The Present: Exploring Greater Quabbin

Dedication

To the former residents of the lost towns, and to Les Campbell who got me started and encouraged me along the way.

Acknowledgements

A great many people helped with this project, sharing their time and knowledge to make this a better book. In particular I'd like to thank Earl Cooley, Lois Barnes, Robert Wilder, Clif Read, Robert Keyes, Les and Terry Campbell, Elizabeth Peirce, and Marty Howe. Several organizations, especially the Metropolitan District Commission, the Friends of the Quabbin, the Swift River Valley Historical Society, the *Union News* of Springfield, The Massachusetts Audubon Society, The Trustees of Reservations and the Massachusetts Department of Fisheries and Wildlife provided guidance and access to their records.

I also wish to thank the many people I interviewed over the past several years, and apologize for any oversights to this list of helpful folks whom I think of as friends: Wendy Anderson, Florence May Avery, Bunny Beardsley, Joe Bergen, Chuck Berube, Jim Cargill, Doris Cargill, Ernie Carrington, Joe Cernauskas, Bob Clark, Douglas Cooley, Lois Cooley, Bill Davis, Wes Dwelly, Jean Ewing, Frank Fallon, Peg Gorman, Ed Hermenau, Richard Hill, Janet Kraft, Jack Lash, Elizabeth Howe Lincoln, Don McMillan, Dale Monette, Bill Pepe, Katherine O'Brien Reed, the Henry Salem family, Irene Stevens, Maude Stone, Jack Swedberg, Bertha Taylor, Mary Thomes, Eugene Tremble, Harrison Thresher, Kip Waugh, Ray Whitaker, and Vernon Vaughn.

Research was greatly enhanced by the helpful assistance of library directors, reference librarians and staff members at more than two dozen libraries. Thank you all.

Finally, I'd like to acknowledge the skillful editing of Adam Gamble, publisher at On Cape Publications. Adam made my writing better without changing my style.

Prologue

Reflections on the Swift River Valley

Imagine owning a farm in the Swift River Valley in the early 1920's and hearing rumors that engineers from Boston were surveying the land, thinking of flooding your town. Preposterous, you think. But the rumors persist and then you see the engineers, tramping your fields, taking measurements, making calculations.

Special town meetings are held, where the powers from Boston outline their plans. They explain that the valley is the ideal place to create a reservoir: clear flowing streams surrounded by high hills. Now the talk is more than rumors and land prices plunge. The politicians assure you fair market value, but they neglect to say they won't cover the demise of your business, your farm, your livelihood. You try to organize your neighbors and put a stop to this nonsense before it gets out of hand. This is America, they cannot just come in and take your home, your land, your town. But the Swift River Valley is a sparsely populated region of farms, mills and small businesses with little political clout. Still, you battle, all the way to the Supreme Court.

Boston wins, however, and now the engineers are joined by loggers. The trees start to come down, and a thick smoke hangs in the air as brush is burned. You get what you can for your home and farm, then watch as your land is stripped and the house that has been in your family for generations is razed. You are not alone; 2,500 other residents are displaced. Even the dead do not escape the injustice; they are dug up and reinterred, all 7,500 souls who thought they might rest in peace in their hometown.

This is what happened to the residents of Dana, Greenwich, Prescott, and Enfield. Maybe the scene I've painted is harsh, but I've listened to the voices of those who were there when this happened. While most of the former residents I talked to were children at the time, the bottom line is that Boston took their towns. They have vivid memories of watching their parents struggle with the fact that even though they owned their lands, their homes, and their businesses, the state evicted them.

When the court battles were over and the exodus of people was in its final days, a Farewell Party and Ball was sponsored by the Enfield Fire Department commemorating "the passing of the town of Enfield and Swift River Valley." *The Springfield Union* chronicled the event, which was held on April 27, 1938, noting, "The orchestra, which had been playing for the firemen's ball throughout the evening, faintly sounded the strain of 'Auld Lang Syne'...muffled sounds of sobbing were heard, hardened men were not ashamed to take out their handkerchiefs."

In a past issue of *Quabbin Voices,* a newsletter put out by the Friends of Quabbin, there was a touching photograph from the Farewell Ball of four people sitting in the upper balcony looking down on the dancers below. The caption read, "Witnesses to the passing of their own history, Enfield's senior citizenry stoically watched a younger generation dance away the final night of the town's existence."

INTRODUCTION

Foreword

When Boston needed more water in the late 1800's and early 1900's, it looked west to the Swift River Valley. The valley had a number of clean rivers and streams, a topography that was perfect for creating a reservoir; and perhaps most important, it was home to a mainly rural population with no cities.

Although some citizen groups from the valley tried to stop the state from taking their towns, the powers aligned against them were simply too strong, and by the late 1920's the first steps toward creating the giant reservoir called Quabbin began. The valley was stripped of trees, homes were razed, and graves were relocated. While the clearing of the valley went on, the construction of the dams began, both the 2,640-foot-long Winsor Dam and the smaller Goodnough Dike. These served to hold back the waters of the Swift River, and for seven years the waters rose until 412 billion gallons covered much of the lost towns.

The towns of Dana, Prescott, Greenwich, and Enfield were wiped off the map. This was not the first time in the region that one group of people took the land from another. During King Philip's War (1675-1676) colonists routed the Nipmuck Indians and took possession of the area. The Nipmucks had lived there for centuries and called the valley Quabbin, or Qaben, which means "place of many waters," or "meeting of the waters." It is an accurate name, because in the valley where the reservoir now rests, the three branches of the Swift River and many smaller streams merged into one. These rivers are the arteries of the Quabbin, pumping it with new life every minute.

The 39-square-mile reservoir is one of the world's largest man-made reservoirs for domestic water supply. Its waters are so pure they are rated "Class A," and they do not require filtration. (Fluoride was added in 1978 for dental health, and small amounts of ammonia and chlorine are added as water enters the final distribution lines.) The reservoir is quite deep, with a maximum depth of 150 feet near the Winsor Dam, and water entering the reservoir can take one to four years to completely circulate the Quabbin, acting as a natural purification process. The Quabbin is a marvel of both man's engineering skills and nature's beauty and simplicity.

The 25,000 acre reservoir has one-hundred and eighteen miles of undeveloped shoreline and is surrounded by 56,000 acres of open space, all within an hour-and-a-half drive from Boston or Providence, and even closer to Springfield, Hartford, and Worcester. While the creation of the Quabbin was

QUABBIN: A HISTORY AND EXPLORER'S GUIDE

tragic to those who once lived there, the silver lining is that the natural habitats created in the process are so pristine that bald eagles and loons nest there, and coyote, fisher, moose, bobcat, and possibly even mountain lion roam the woods.

* * *

What I refer to as the Greater Quabbin Region is much more than the reservoir and its protected watershed. It's an area of handsome towns with an extraordinary amount of conservation land, with fascinating points of interest scattered through-out the countryside. It's a region to visit time and again, to view wildlife, walk, bike, hike, canoe, or to cruise the backroads in search of history and relaxation.

If you only explore the Winsor Dam, Goodnough Dike, and Visitor Center, you are missing the full measure of what the region has to offer. Besides the many access points to the reservoir (called "gates"), the nearby towns should also be investigated. Such points of interest as the Bear's Den, Royalston Falls, the Rockingstone, North Common Meadow, the Rock House Reservation, the Swift River Valley Historical Society museums, and hundreds of other special places entice the explorer.

This book is divided into two main sections: the first covers the history of the valley and the construction of the reservoir, while the second section is an explorer's guide. For first time visitors, I suggest reading the "Quick Guide" chapter, and selecting an area for an initial trip. Whether your passion is history or wildlife, the Quick Guide will give you a thumbnail sketch of interesting sites. For those readers that have a particular field of interest, go straight to the chapter of your choice. There are chapters on hiking, wildlife, fishing, biking/backroading, and more.

Quabbin is a treasure, and my hope is that all who visit it will do so with respect.

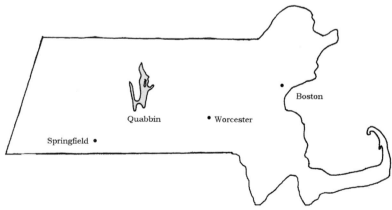

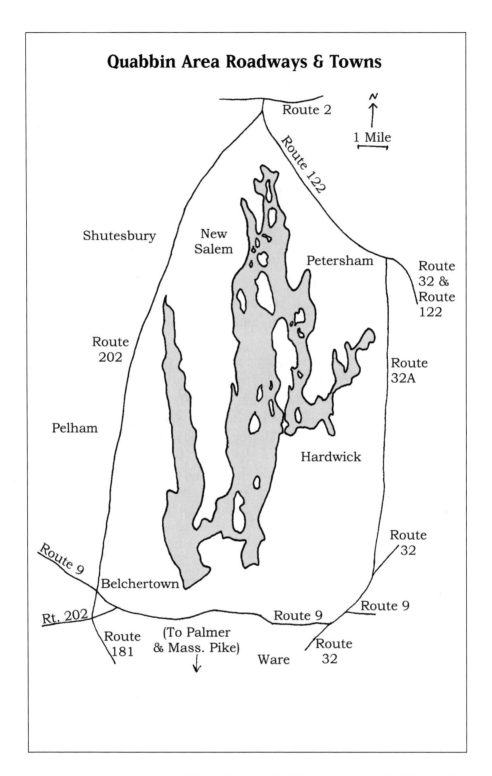

Quabbin Area Roadways & Towns

Route 2

N
1 Mile

Route 122

Shutesbury

New Salem

Petersham

Route 32 & Route 122

Route 202

Route 32A

Pelham

Hardwick

Route 9

Route 32

Belchertown

Rt. 202

Route 9

Route 9

Route 181

(To Palmer & Mass. Pike)

Route 32

Ware

Quabbin Facts and Figures

(Source: Metropolitan District Commission)

Reservoir length: 18 miles
Reservoir maximum depth: 151 feet
Average reservoir depth: 45 feet
Reservoir shoreline without islands: 118 miles
Island shoreline: 63 miles
Reservoir capacity: 412 billion gallons
Reservoir surface area: 25,000 acres
Top one inch when full: 750 million gallons
Quabbin watershed area: 120,000 acres
MDC-owned land and water: 81,000
Prescott Peninsula: 12,300 acres
Islands: 3,500 acres
Towns in watershed: Athol, Barre, Belchertown, Hardwick, New Salem,
Orange, Pelham, Petersham, Phillipston, Shutesbury, Ware, Wendell
Swift River minimum release: 20 million gallons per day
Average annual precipitation: 44 inches
Average precipitation yield to reservoir: 50%
Average reservoir gain from one-inch precipitation: 1.6 billion gallons

Communities Served by the Quabbin

(2.5 million people receive water from the Quabbin)

Arlington	Framingham*	Melrose	Somerville	Wilbraham
Bedford	Leominster*	Milton	Southborough	Winchester*
Belmont	Lexington	Nahant	S. Hadley Fire District	Winthrop
Boston	Lynnfield	Needham*	Stoneham	Woburn*
Brookline	Water	Newton	Swampscott	Worcester*
Cambridge*	District	Northborough*	Wakefield*	*partially supplied
Canton*	Lynn*	Norwood	Waltham	
Chelsea	Malden	Peabody*	Watertown	
Chicopee	Marblehead	Quincy	Wellesley*	
Clinton	Marlborough*	Revere	Weston	
Everett	Medford	Saugus		

THE PAST, PART I
Creating the Quabbin

Metropolitan Boston's Expanding Water Sources

(Source: Friends of the Quabbin & MDC)

As early Boston's population grew, the city diverted water via aqueducts from farther and farther away, primarily from lakes, rivers, and man-made reservoirs to the west. The following is a brief chronology of when additional water sources were acquired.

1795: Jamaica Pond in Roxbury

1848: Lake Cochituate in Natick

1870: Water from the Sudbury River is diverted to Lake Cochituate.

1878: Construction of the Sudbury Reservoir is completed, connecting it to Lake Cochituate through a 17.4-mile aqueduct.

1880: Framingham reservoirs are added to the metropolitan area water supply.

1893: More water is needed and the Massachusetts Board of Health considers Lake Winnipesaukee in New Hampshire, Sebago Lake in Maine, the Merrimac River, and the Nashua River. The Nashua River is selected to create Wachusett Reservoir.

1895: Construction of the Wachusett Reservoir begins.

1895: Initial surveys of the Swift River conducted.

1908: Wachusett Reservoir completed, and at the time is the largest man-made drinking water reservoir in the world.

1919: Metropolitan District Water Supply Commission created, and studies begin to focus on the Millers, Swift and Ware Rivers as additional water sources. These studies prove to be the beginning of the end for the Swift River Valley.

Building the Quabbin
and How It Works

As the population of Boston grew by 50% from 1890 to 1920, its water supply, primarily from Lake Cochituate and the Wachusett Reservoir, did not keep pace. Commissions began to address the issue, and they looked westward to both the Ware and Swift rivers for additional water.

The Ware River was analyzed because it was only 12 miles from the Wachusett Reservoir, while the Swift River Valley was attractive to engineers because of its many rivers and surrounding topography. X.H. Goodnough, an engineer from Boston who enjoyed trout fishing in the Swift River Valley, was one of the first to note that the high hills surrounding the water-rich valley would make a natural boundary for a reservoir. He recognized that the bowl-shaped valley had only two major gaps at the southern end which could be dammed to form a giant reservoir. Other engineers soon noticed similar features of the valley. Frederick Stearns, an engineer with the Massachusetts State Board of Health, noted that the Swift River was pure and clear, and that "the streams have very little fall and the valleys are wide."

The first study of the Swift River was completed in 1895, when a brief survey was undertaken focusing on the river's flow and area elevations. Rumors soon started circulating about the demise of the valley, and property values began dropping soon after, followed by several years of uncertainty for the people who lived there. Some immediately began to move, but many more thought the reservoir, which was discussed for years, would never actually be built.

A second survey was conducted in 1921 focusing on the feasibility of a reservoir and its linkage to Boston. In 1922 a joint report of the Metropolitan District Water Supply Commission[1] and the Massachusetts State Board of Health was filed, calling for the creation of a massive reservoir that would be fed by both the Swift and the Ware rivers. This proposal would become the basis for the state acts that followed. First, the Ware River Act was passed in

---

[1] The functions of the Metropolitan District Water Supply Commission were transfered to the Metropolitan District Commission in 1947. The functions did not change, however, and for clarity the author will use the term Commission when refering to either entity.

1926 allowing for the construction of a tunnel to divert water from the Ware River to the Wachusett Reservoir. This was followed by the Swift River Act of 1927, which appropriated 65 million dollars for the taking of the Swift River Valley and the creation of the Quabbin Reservoir.

Frank E. Winsor was appointed Chief Engineer of the Quabbin Project, and initial construction began in 1927. Of note is the fact that Winsor died in 1939 and never saw the completion of the project. His death from a heart attack occurred while he was testifying in a court case regarding a Quabbin contractor.

While the Quabbin was being constructed, the water in the Wachusett Reservoir had dropped to critical levels, and construction of the portion of the Quabbin Aqueduct from the Ware River to the Wachusett Reservoir was made a priority. In 1931, a year when the Wachusett Reservoir was only at 19% of capacity, this portion of the aqueduct was completed and diversions from the Ware River to the Wachusett Reservoir began.

The Winsor Dam and Goodnough Dike

The key to creating the Quabbin was the impoundment structures, now known as the Winsor Dam and Goodnough Dike, named after engineers Frank Winsor and Xavier Goodnough. The dam and dike were built by sealing their base on the valley floor with a row of caissons attached to bedrock. (A caisson is a hollow, rectangular-shaped, pressurized watertight cement chamber, approximately 45 feet in length and nine feet in width.) The caissons were open at the top and bottom. Beneath each initial section of caisson was a similarly shaped steel box called a cutting shoe, approximately six feet high. Men worked in the caissons excavating rock and earth, but did so in short shifts to avoid getting the bends. Compressed air was sent into these caisson chambers to keep ground water out.

As earth was removed by buckets on ropes, the caissons and the cutting shoes settled deeper. Additional sections of a caisson were added once the initial caisson section and cutting shoe settled below the original valley floor. Forty caissons were sunk at the Winsor Dam, and 37 were sunk at the dike. The caissons at the Winsor Dam reached solid ledge with no ground water seepage at 125 feet below the level of the Swift River. Once the caissons were at bedrock they were then filled with concrete and sealed to both the valley floor and adjacent caissons, forming a core wall along the length of the dam and dike. An impervious hydraulic fill of fine sand was packed along the sides of the caissons, and more cement was poured across their tops.

Another key to the strength of the dam and dike is their sloping "A" shape. The Winsor Dam is 35 feet wide at its top, but at its bottom widens to 724 feet. Four million cubic yards of fill were used in its formation. In 1938 *The Springfield Union* described this process, reporting, "A novel manner of placing this earth has been developed by the contractor. The hydraulic fill is placed by gravity flow from a high level hog box, fed by a series of belt conveyers from three borrow pits. The dry material is mixed with water, pumped from the river, for gravity flow to discharge lines along the upstream and downstream beaches or margins of the dam." To better understand this technique, picture the top of the emerging dam as trough-shaped, with the two outer edges higher than the center. The soil and water mixture was sluiced down from the "hog-box" and slowly released along the top of the dam's two edges. The coarse soil settled more quickly at the outer fringes of the dam, while fine soil, the most impervious to water, settled at the center of the dam making it watertight.

The downstream side of the Winsor Dam was covered with soil, forming a long slope, while the upstream side of the dam was covered with a rip rap of stone, forming a similarly sized slope (most of which is now under water). During construction a small railroad was built to carry the boulders to this upstream side. First, smaller rocks were laid, followed by larger boulders, to prevent erosion from waves. (The Quabbin gets some large waves on stormy days, which is one reason canoes are not allowed on the reservoir.)

The larger of the two impoundment structures, the Winsor Dam (2,640 feet long and 295 feet high including the depth of the caissons), was constructed with both a spillway and a diversion tunnel. The spillway allows excess water to leave the reservoir when it exceeds its capacity of 412 billion gallons. The reservoir has only flowed over the spillway approximately 40% of the years since its first overflow in 1946. You can see the handsome arch of the spillway at the east end of the dam. (Where the spillway corridor meets the released waters from the outlet building, a "Y-Pool" is formed, a favorite of fly-fishermen. (See the chapter "Fishing in and Around the Quabbin" at the end of this book for more information.) A second, auxiliary spillway was also constructed on the west side of the dam. It was built for emergencies and has never been used.

Below the Winsor Dam is the diversion tunnel for the Swift River, which had carried the river downstream while the dam was being built. Water continues to flow through the tunnel at a minimum rate of 20 million gallons per day into the Swift River streambed south of the dam. The state of Connecticut had brought suit against Massachusetts regarding riparian rights to the river, and in the set-

Quabbin and Wachusett Aqueduct System

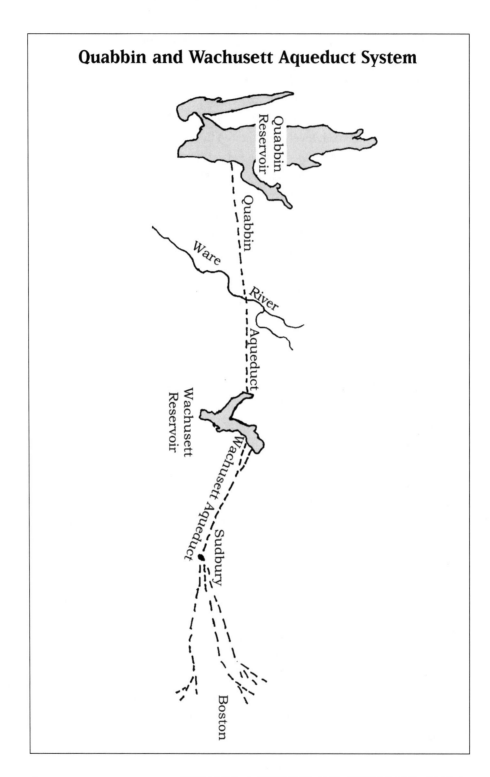

tlement the minimum flow was established. The release of water formerly generated electricity which was then sold to local power companies and used to power the Metropolitan District Commission's administration building. You can see where this water exits the reservoir below the dam through what is called the Outlet Building. An access road, now closed to vehicles, leads from the dam to the Outlet Building. This Outlet Building also diverts water to the Chicopee Valley Aqueduct, which then delivers it to Chicopee, Wilbraham, and parts of South Hadley, the only communities in Western Massachusetts that get water from the Quabbin.

When the Winsor Dam was being constructed, a space was built for an airplane hanger at the dam's base on the reservoir side. The idea was to have a floatplane patrol the Quabbin and also serve as a form of transportation for officials from Boston, but later it was decided to use boats for patrolling the reservoir. A large patrol boat and some heavy equipment now occupy the hanger. The maximum depth of the reservoir-151 feet-occurs directly in front of Winsor Dam. The average depth of the reservoir is 51 feet.

The Goodnough Dike (2,140 feet long and 135 feet high) is called a dike rather than a dam because unlike a dam it holds back all the water, and there is no spillway or release tunnel. The Goodnough Dike's construction is similar to the Winsor Dam, and it is situated about two miles northeast as the crow flies.

As progress on the reservoir's construction continued, thousands of people, primarily from Springfield, Hartford and Worcester, would drive out for a look. The interest in the Quabbin was so great that *The Springfield Union* began a series entitled, "Letters From Quabbin," which appeared twice a week for four months in 1938. Written by Mabel Jones and Amy Spink, both former residents of Greenwich, the letters served as both an update to the public regarding construction at the Quabbin, as well as an eyewitness account of the final days of the community.

The Aqueduct

Before and during construction of the dams, an underground aqueduct (12 feet 9 inches high and 11 feet wide) was built to bring the water to Boston. The aqueduct, bored into bedrock and lined with cement, makes a relatively straight line from the Quabbin Reservoir to the Wachusett Reservoir, covering a distance of 24.6 miles and making it one of the longest tunnels in the world. (It is only a half-mile shorter than the Hetch-Hetchy in California.) Along the way it passes the Ware River, where, during low water periods, water from the river can be divert-

Excavating rock inside the underground aqueduct was the most dangerous job during construction of the Quabbin. The 24-mile underground aqueduct, which carries water from Quabbin to Wachusett, has a maximum depth of 650 feet.

ed into the aqueduct by dropping 259 feet through the Ware River Intake to the Quabbin Aqueduct. However, when this is done, the flow in the aqueduct is temporarily reversed, so that the water from the river first goes into the Quabbin. Water from the river is thereby purified through circulation with water already in the Quabbin. Water from the Ware River can only be diverted from October 15th to June 15th and only when the river flow exceeds 85 million gallons per day.

Water from the Quabbin enters the aqueduct on its journey toward Boston via Shaft 12 on the east side of the reservoir. One problem that had to be solved was that the Ware River enters the Quabbin via a diversion tunnel at a point close to Shaft 12, and this Ware River water might not have a chance to become fully integrated into the reservoir before being siphoned off toward Boston. The problem was solved by the construction of the north and south baffle dams that separate the Ware River's entry point from Shaft 12. These baffle dams were built at the former site of Greenwich Village and were given the name "baffle" because they changed the direction of the water flow. The baffle dams were quite ingenious because only a couple of relatively small dams were needed to force the water of the Ware River to flow far to the north, away from Shaft 12. The south dam connects the main shoreline with a small island; and the larger north dam (1,615 feet long) connects this island with the Quabbin's largest island, Mount Zion, creating a long finger of land that the Ware River water must circulate around. This allows the sediment of the Ware River to be filtered out and its natural tea-coloration to mix with the other reservoir water.

Shaft 12, located about half-way up the reservoir on the east side and presently closed to the public, is one of 13 shafts that provide entry points into the aqueduct. During construction excavated earth and rock were removed through these shafts. In some spots, excavated rock was made into concrete at plants built near the shafts. The overall depth of the aqueduct ranges from 657 feet at Shaft 5 in Rutland to 262 feet at Shaft 8 in Coldbrook. Although many people think it takes days for water to travel through the aqueduct from Quabbin to Wachusett, it only takes 6 to 12 hours, and a maximum capacity of 600 million gallons a day can be moved. Water was first diverted from Quabbin to Wachusett in 1941, well before the reservoir had filled, due to Boston's acute need for more water.

Because the Quabbin's elevation of 530 feet is higher than that of Boston's, gravity is the primary mechanism that propels the water through the aqueduct. Along the way, the flow of water produces small amounts of electricity generated at various stations.

Although largely forgotten, the construction of the Ware River intake and the protection of the Ware River Watershed caused several villages to be abandoned and demolished. Sections of Barre, Hubbardston, Oakham and Rutland

Once the aqueduct was tunneled through bedrock it was lined with concrete.

were all taken over by the Commission. Casualties included private homes, mills, and a state prison camp in Rutland. The village of Coldbrook Springs in Oakham was the largest village to be demolished, with approximately 30 homes razed or moved and 100 people affected. Coldbrook Springs was known for its mineral springs which people bathed in believing the waters had therapeutic powers for many ailments. In addition to the private homes, the village also had a post office, a general store, and a forty-room hotel.

Clearing the Valley

The land to be covered by the Quabbin was totally stripped of trees and every building was moved or torn down. All vegetation was to be removed to a height of 10 feet above the flood line. The tops of the hills within the valley—which would become islands—were left wooded. Special bulldozers uprooted small trees and brush which was pushed into piles and burned. Don McMillan, who lived in Hardwick and did not have to leave his home, still has one clear memory of the construction and clearing of the valley in Greenwich. "We would sit on the porch of our house and the western sky was aglow at night from the flames of the burning brush in the valley. It was eerie," he said.

Unemployed workers throughout Massachusetts made their way to Quabbin hoping for work. Most of the tree cutting jobs, however, were used as a political tool by Governor James Michael Curley, who let Boston politicians give them to men in their district in exchange for supporting Curley's budget at the State House. People from the valley derisively called these woodcutters the "wood-

Enfield before the clearing of the valley, looking northwesterly. Mount Ram at the end of the Prescott Peninsula is in the background.

QUABBIN: A HISTORY AND EXPLORER'S GUIDE

peckers," knowing full well most of them had never handled an axe. Even the woodpeckers themselves knew they were the beneficiaries of patronage, referring to their enterprise as "Curley's Summer Camp."

During the summer of 1936 the clearing of the valley began in earnest, when 3,000 woodpeckers worked six- and seven-day weeks. They did receive one unusual holiday, however: a day off when they were encouraged to head back to Boston to vote in the Massachusetts primary election! The woodpeckers were accused of stealing tools and doing only a fourth of the work a professional logger could do in a day. One woodpecker was killed when a tree fell on him. As one might expect with 3,000 young men housed away from home, there were many charges of public drunkenness and disorderly conduct at night in towns like Ware, Palmer and Belchertown, where most of them lived.

A few years ago I had the good fortune to interview Frank Fallon, who was once a woodpecker during construction of the Quabbin, and he eloquently recalled the experience:

"I was instructed to cut the trees as close to the ground as possible. We used two-man saws and were in the woods all day. I was a city boy from Dorchester, a real greenhorn, but I really took to the woods. While I was working out there I boarded in Belchertown, and I fell in love with a local girl. It was the happiest year of my life! I had work during the Depression, I enjoyed being outdoors, and I had my girl. But it was in stark contrast to some of the people who had to give up their homes—some of them never recovered emotionally."

CREATING THE QUABBIN

The town is reduced to rubble. Note that the trees on Mount Ram have not been cut because those were to be above the waterline. (Photo taken 1939 from the rear of the Chandler Building.)

QUABBIN: A HISTORY AND EXPLORER'S GUIDE

Beside the timber that the Quabbin woodcutters removed, the powerful Hurricane of 1938 blew down 50 million board feet of timber. The hurricane followed nine straight days of rain which exacerbated the situation. Although 11.6 inches of rain fell in just five days, no damage was done to the dams. Most of the downed timber was salvaged, reducing fire hazards and raising revenues to offset costs.

As families moved out of the valley after selling their homes to the Commission, some of these homes were allowed to stand for a few years and were rented to needy families. There was no shortage of unemployed city people during the Great Depression, and they welcomed the chance to rent a house (sometimes complete with farm) for about $5 a month. Of course, these renters eventually also moved out as the valley was cleared.

Most homes were torn down and the lumber sold, but a fair number were moved, often by cutting them into halves or thirds and transported by truck. A speculator purchased several valley structures and had them moved to Dorset, Vermont where wealthy New Yorkers bought them as summer homes. Buildings that had not been torn down for lumber or moved were often bulldozed into their own cellar holes. (Walking through the reservation today one often happens upon a cellar hole, with cement or stone steps still intact leading up to what was once the front door.)

In 1938, the woodpeckers, as well as some privately contracted loggers and bulldozers, went through the valley one last time to clear the remaining brush that might produce algae in the coming reservoir. At the same time trees were cut down within the parameters of the coming reservoir, millions of seedlings, mostly evergreens, were planted above the high-water mark in open fields surrounding the reservoir to serve as a buffer zone and prevent erosion. Red pines were the most common seedling planted, but this later proved to be a bad choice because they consumed lots of water. During the past few years the MDC has removed many of the red pines.

In addition to the removal of trees and 650 homes, 7,561 bodies previously buried in 34 cemeteries (13 public cemeteries and 21 private sites) within the reservation were moved. The majority, approximately 6,500, were reinterred at the Quabbin Park Cemetery while the remainder went to other cemeteries. Thirty-six miles of state highway were relocated and 31 miles of railroad tracks dismantled. But the figure that really matters is the 2,500 people who were forced to relocate from their homes.

This shot, taken in October of 1939, shows the Quabbin filling just two months after the diversion tunnel was blocked. It took seven years for the entire reservoir to fill. The photo was taken from the West Traffic Circle at the Winsor Dam.

Completion

In August of 1938 the last few residents were ordered out of the valley and roads leading into the valley were closed, with all public access to them denied. Finally, in 1939 the project was completed. On August 14th the diversion tunnel that carried the Swift River through the Winsor Dam was blocked and the water began to rise. It took seven years for the entire reservoir to fill, covering 25,000 acres of the valley. The first water was released over the Winsor Dam Spillway at a special ceremony on June 22, 1946. Amazingly, only 53 million of the 65 million dollars appropriated for construction was spent, largely because of cheap Depression era wages. But construction of the reservoir and the aqueducts also had a cost in human lives—26 men died in accidents; approximately half were killed while constructing the aqueduct.

After the reservoir's completion, water demands on the Quabbin and the MDC system grew steadily each year until 1989 when the MDC, the Massachusetts Water Resources Authority, and the Department of Environmental Protection declared an emergency which resulted in a program to expand leak detection, conserve water, and increase water prices. This resulted in a drop in consumption from 330 million gallons a day in 1989 to 250 million gallons by 1995. Prior to the success of this program, consideration was given to diverting water from the Connecticut River into the Quabbin. The plan called for pumping Connecticut River water to a holding reservoir at Northfield Mountain and then carrying it via aqueducts to the Quabbin. Although this never got off the drawing board, in a sense Boston is already getting water that was originally intended for the Connecticut River, because both the Ware River and the Swift River feed the Chicopee River which in turn feeds the Connecticut.

Today, the Quabbin supplies 2.5 million people with water. Besides Boston, 45 other towns receive drinking water from the reservoir. Most of the towns are clustered around Boston, with Marblehead, Peabody and Lynnfield to the north, Lexington, Weston and Wellesley to the west, and Norwood, Canton and Quincy to the south.

It should be noted the Quabbin concept is not appropriate for every state. I was recently in Florida where I came across a letter to the editor of a local newspaper touting a massive reservoir as the solution to Florida's water problem. The letter used Quabbin as an example. One problem with this idea is that Florida does not have sizable hills, while the Swift River Valley was walled in by hills 400 to 600 feet in height, providing a readymade "bowl" that only had to be damned at its southern end.

The first water was released over the spillway on June 22, 1946.

This view taken from the Enfield Lookout in late 1938 or 1939 shows the reservoir just beginning to fill.

QUABBIN: A HISTORY AND EXPLORER'S GUIDE

Quabbin Milestones, Forgotten Events and Notes

- Most of the hearings regarding the proposed building of the reservoir were held in Boston rather than in the valley. Residents of the doomed towns, who had little political clout, had a difficult time getting to the meetings, with automobile driving speeds at a mere 20 miles an hour and a train ride taking the better part of a day

- In 1928, after the state approved the Swift River Act, there were still concerns regarding the viability of the Quabbin. The Springfield Union ran an article in which Chairman Davis B. Keniston of the Metropolitan Water Supply Commission "admitted there is an engineering question whether the Swift River in and of itself would fill a reservoir as extensive as that proposed." The article went on to say, "Now the question is being asked why should $50,000,000 be spent on a plan so expansive that it never could be fully utilized unless other rivers in that part of the Commonwealth could later be seized to fill it."

- A group of citizens from Boston, known as the Metropolitan Improvement Association, wanted to name Quabbin the Calvin Coolidge Reservoir after Coolidge, who died in 1933.

- During construction a proposal was made to build a four million dollar bridge and highway across the reservoir.

- In 1935 a highway running along the west side of the reservoir was opened and named after Daniel Shays, leader of the rebellion which occurred in Massachusetts just after the Revolutionary War. That same year, the last run of the Springfield to Athol train occurred.

- At two different time periods the Quabbin was used for military training. During World War II the Quabbin was used for low-level training flights and bombing practice by the Army Air Corps out of Westover Air Force Base. At that time the Quabbin was still filling and the bombing targets were in a section of North Dana that had been cleared but not yet underwater. Observation towers, with communication wire running among them, were erected along what would become the shoreline. Rather than using live ammunition, the Army Air Corps used sand-filled canisters, approximately a foot in diameter. An occasional rusted canister, dropped inaccurately from a plane, can still be found crushed like an accordion in the woods.

During the Korean War, 20-millimeter cannons were tested near the Goodnough Dike by firing them at Little Quabbin Mountain. Bob Clark, President of the Friends of Quabbin, recalls that these rapid-fire cannons, which were later mounted on planes, could be heard echoing off the hills all the way to his home in Petersham.

• The dam and dike area were first opened to the public in 1945. Shoreline fishing was first allowed in 1946 and boat fishing in 1952.

• The Chicopee Aqueduct was completed in 1950, transporting Quabbin water to Wilbraham and Chicopee, and later to a portion of South Hadley.

• A radio astronomy telescope facility was built on Prescott Peninsula in 1969.

• Quabbin was at its lowest level (45%) in 1967, while its highest level (103%) occurred in 1984. The minimum capacity to ensure water quality is 38%.

Cemeteries:
Removing 7,500 Dead

Every gravesite within the Quabbin Reservoir Reservation had to be excavated and the bodies removed and re-buried outside the reservoir prior to the flooding of the valley. The majority of the deceased were reinterred at the specially designated Quabbin Park Cemetery located on Route 9 in Ware, not far from the Quabbin Visitor Center. Like most other aspects about the Quabbin, rumors flew at the time. One spreading rumor, which was completely false, was that laborers who signed up to remove the bodies would be paid unbelievably high wages and be housed in exceptionally fine living conditions.

A total of 7,561 bodies were removed; 6,551 went to the Quabbin Park Cemetery while the remaining 1,010 were reinterred at other cemeteries. The first removals began in 1928. The Metropolitan District Water Supply Commission* estimated the cost to be $18 per body for those that went to the Quabbin Park Cemetery, and $31 per body for those sent elsewhere. For families that wished to purchase a lot outside the Quabbin Park Cemetery, the Commission would provide a maximum payment of $35 which was the estimated value of a lot at the Quabbin Park Cemetery.

The Springfield Union reported, "Most of the bodies moved to places other than Quabbin Park were taken in the earlier years. Since the beauty of the new cemetery has become so obvious, however, and the management so efficient, few request are made now [1938] for any other location."

Before removing a body, authorities first photographed each lot in the cemeteries and all available data were recorded. Families holding deeds were notified, and they in turn selected a location in the new cemetery. Assistant Engineer William Potter was in charge of the removal of bodies and was assisted by undertaker Clifton Moore, a native of Enfield who gave up his business to help coordinate the project. Having a local undertaker supervising this process must have allayed the fears of valley residents that the remains of their loved ones would not be handled with respect and theft of items would occur.

The Springfield Union reported that when a lot was transferred, "the stones or monuments are first removed and set on solid foundations in the new location:

then the laborers remove the earth carefully from the grave until the body is reached. The undertaker then removes the body, the remains being placed in covered wooden boxes. Any articles of jewelry or the like, found in the graves, is recorded and buried with the one to whom it belongs. The bodies are carried in a hearse kept for that purpose only." Many of the old graves were unmarked, and more than 500 nameless bodies were removed, some from "potter's fields."

Author James Christenson reported in the *Journal of the New England Water Works Association* that the condition of the coffin, clothing and physical frame of the deceased was completely disintegrated in most cases. The skull and principal parts of the skeleton, however, were usually intact. "The entire remains were collected in wooden boxes, great care being used to discover and save every remaining element of the skeletal structure. This was then mixed with soil from its immediate vicinity and the box closed," Christenson reported.

Public Memorials from the abandoned towns were reset in the memorial section of the Quabbin Park Cemetery. These included the Enfield Civil War Monument and cannon, the Prescott Monument donated by John Atkinson, the Ballou Monument, and the War Memorial and cannon from Dana. A stone monument to the people of Greenwich, donated by Harrison Thresher, was erected at the Quabbin Park Cemetery in 2000.

One last note of interest is the case of an overlooked grave within the Quabbin Reservation. Elizabeth Peirce, President of the Swift River Valley Historical Society, informed me that one grave above the Quabbin water line within the reservation was not moved. The burial site is that of a six-year-old boy. It was located in a private site rather than a cemetery, and the headstone was discovered by a hiker.

If You Go

Quabbin Park Cemetery is located on the south side of Route 9 in Ware, just east of the main entrance to the Visitor Center and Winsor Dam.

The headstone of Deacon James Wright, who died in 1754, is the oldest stone in the Quabbin Park Cemetery. Another old headstone for Elizabeth Ann Cutler, who died in 1774, is inscribed as follows: "Suddenly departed this life in a apoplectic fit. Death cuts off all, both great and small."

• Control of the Quabbin Park Cemetery was under the Metropolitan District Water Supply Commission until that organization expired and control was passed to the Metropolitan District Commission.

Negotiating the
Sale of Property

Writing in the *Journal of the New England Water Works Association* in 1945, James Christenson outlined the procedures used by residents and the Commission for the transfer of property. He explained that the sale of most property, and the value assigned to property, occurred through negotiation. Property owners would complete an owner's declaration form with an offer to sell at a set price. The Commission would then assign three appraisers to investigate and make an independent appraisal of the property. Using this information, the Commission's purchasing agent would negotiate with the owner until an agreed-upon price was reached. The first offer was received on October 21, 1926 from Alice G. Parsons who owned property in Enfield and Greenwich. Occasionally, the negotiations would reach an impass and would be decided by the courts.

Because the building of the aqueduct and the Ware River diversion needed to be done as quickly as possible to alleviate Boston's water shortage, the purchases of properties lying within that construction area were done aggressively.

Copies of the forms and the final notice to the towns are shown on the following pages in this order:

• Property Owner's Declaration Form and Offer to Sell

• Appraiser's Property Report

• Notice to the Towns of Disincorporation

Reproduction of property owner's declaration form and offer to sell.

Property Blank
(Form No. 28)

To the Metropolitan District Water Supply Commission:

The undersigned is the owner of the real estat on_____ Street
in the town of_____ Distant_____miles from
_____ Nearest Village, Post Office or Railroad Station,
consisting of _____acres of land and the following buildings thereon:
_____room house, about _____ years old. (Street number_____)

(Describe any other buildings)

Of said land_____ acres is tillable:_____ acres woodland.
Estimated value of wood and timber, $_____
I acquired title to said property, from_____
By deed dated_____recorded with_____
Deeds, book_____ page_____ The price paid by me was$_____
There is a first mortgage on the property, held by_____
Upon which there is a balance due of $_____

(Give full particulars as to any other mortgages)

The property was assessed in

193___	193___	193___
land $_____	land $_____	land$_____
buildings $_____	buildings $_____	buildings$_____
total $_____	total $_____	total$_____

There has been expended for improvements during the last five years the
following amounts: (State nature of improvements)

The property is occupied by_____
There is a lease for_____years, expiring on the _____day of _____,___
The rent received is $_____ per year.

I am willing to sell the above property to the Commonwealth for $_____
I desire to continue to occupy the premises until_____
Other information:

Date_____

_____
Signature of Owner

Address_____

Reproduction of part of the form used for the Appraiser's Property Report.

Metropolitan District Water Supply Commission
Appraiser's Property Report
(Form No. 129)

Property of _____ on_____Street,
Town of _____, Distant_____miles from
_____Nearest Village, Post Office or Railroad Station.
Mark location of property on map on reverse side of this page.
Address of Owner_____
Use of property (residence, farm, woodland, etc.)_____
Does owner occupy premises?_____
Area of land:____ acres tillage; _____ pasture; ____ woodland ;____ total ;____
Description of buildings (Age, condition, and improvements)
Water rights:
Mortgates:

      First Mortgage: Mortgagee _____Amount_____Bal. Due_____
      Other Mortgage: Mortgagee_____Amount_____Bal. Due_____
Names of tenants:
Rents now and formerly paid by tenants:
Has tenant a written lease, if so, date of same_____
      Date of expiration of lease_____
Property acquired from_____ Date_____
      Amount paid_____ Date of Deed_____
      Deed Recorded County_____ Book_____ Page_____
Improvements made during last five years:

Property assessed,   193 ,   land $_____
                                   buildings $_____
                                   total $_____

                    193 ,   land $_____
                                   buildings $_____
                                   total $ _____

                    193 ,   land $_____
                                   buildings $_____
                                   total $_____
What does owner want for property?
Your estimate, value of land   tillage $_____
                                   pasture $_____
                                   woodland$_____
                                   buildings $_____
                                   Total Property $_____

Is property salable other than for water works purposes?
Do you recommend purchase with or without timber and buildings?
How long does tenant desire to remain in possession?
Reasons for valuation and other information for Commission:

Signature_____
                 Appraiser.

Reproduction of notice informing Dana, Enfield, Greenwich and Prescott that they were no longer in existence.

Metropolitan District Water Supply Commission
20 Somerset Street, Boston, Massachusetts

April 28, 1938

To All former Town Officers of Towns of Enfield, Greenwich, Dana and Prescott:

By the terms of Chapter 321, Act 1927, as amended by Chapter 240 of the Acts and Resolves of the Legislature of the year 1938, you are herby formally notified that the corporate existence of the aforesaid towns ceased at 12 o'clock midnight, April 27th.

In view of this fact, the town's officers are to carry on no municipal functions on and after April 27th and shall do only such acts as are necessary to effect the transfer of properties of the municipalities to the Metropolitan District Water Supply Commission and to effect the commitment of taxes to the towns to which the respective territories are annexed.

Met. Dist. Water Supply Com.
R. Nelson Molt
Secretary

THE PAST, PART II
The Lost Towns

The Lost Towns

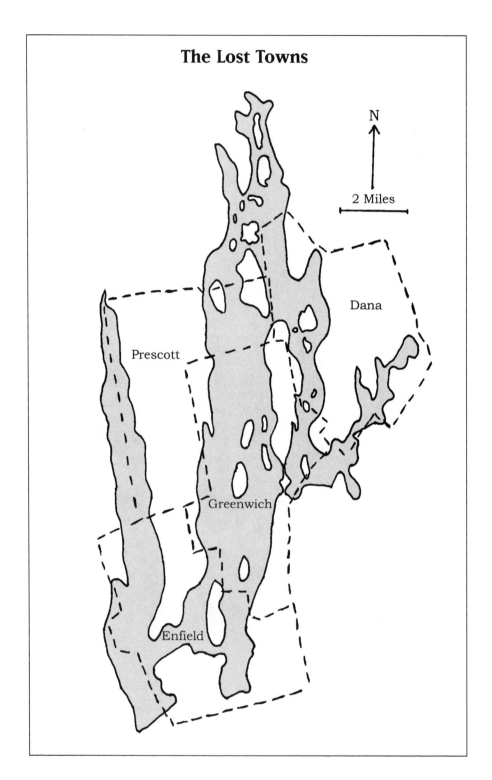

N

2 Miles

Dana

Prescott

Greenwich

Enfield

QUABBIN: A HISTORY AND EXPLORER'S GUIDE

Prescott

Prescott had the smallest population of the four lost towns. Its number of residents peaked at 700-800 in the early 1800's and declined to about 300 in 1900. Most of Prescott's residents worked on farms, and almost all of the land was fields, pastures and orchards by 1830. Prescott's few businesses included a cheese factory, grist mills, charcoal kilns, and a match manufacturer. Soapstone was also mined to use in the manufacturing of sinks.

Prescott was named for Colonel William Prescott who commanded the American forces at Bunker Hill. The town was comprised of three small villages, each surrounded by scattered homesteads. In the town's northern section was North Prescott (near Gate 20); in the center was Atkinson Hollow; and to the south was Prescott Hill which was considered the main village. Most of Prescott was located on rolling hills with much of it on a ridge that ran between the Middle and West Branches of the Swift River. Rattlesnake Mountain, named when a den of rattlesnakes was found at its base, rose abruptly on the west side of the town.

Prescott was incorporated rather late for the region, in 1822, from sections of Pelham and New Salem. Ironically, when Prescott was disincorporated, some of its land outside the boundaries established for the reservation was given back to New Salem. The Commission actually began running Prescott's affairs in 1928, because many residents had sold their land to the Commission in the preceding years. Although many people think Prescott was the first of the lost towns to be disincorporated, former resident Lois Barnes reports that the Commission opted to delay disincorporation until the Quabbin project was completed because of the need to change the county lines as well as the town lines. (The area of Prescott that is now located in New Salem is presently part of Franklin County instead of Hampshire County.) Lois told me that the interim affairs of Prescott were administered by former town officials including her parents. "During the national elections in 1932 and 1936," said Lois, "my parents had to set up a polling place in Prescott even though there were probably less than three voters living in the town."

As was the case with the other lost towns, most buildings were torn down for lumber and few were moved. As mentioned earlier, many were purchased by

Prescott had the fewest residents of any of the lost towns. Prescott was quite hilly — **perhaps this hunter was headed for the hills with his hounds.**

QUABBIN: A HISTORY AND EXPLORER'S GUIDE

a speculator and relocated to Dorset, Vermont to be used as summer homes for vacationing New Yorkers. The Prescott Methodist Church, however, was purchased for $5 by the Prescott Historical Society; it now stands as a museum on the grounds of the Swift River Historical Society in New Salem. Another Prescott church, the Prescott Hill Congregational Church, was moved to Route 116 in South Hadley. The Prescott Town Hall was relocated to Petersham, and the Atkinson Tavern was moved to the grounds of the Storrowtown Tavern in West Springfield.

(It's important to note that besides Prescott and the other three lost towns, eight neighboring communities also lost land to the Quabbin. Those towns were Pelham, New Salem, Shutesbury, Belchertown, Ware, Hardwick, Petersham and Barre.)

Prescott Pilgrimage

Like a long finger, the Prescott Peninsula protrudes into the Quabbin Reservoir, with the tip of the finger almost reaching the Winsor Dam. From Gate 17 at Route 202, it's about 10 and a half miles to the tip, and the peninsula includes sections of two lost towns: Prescott and Enfield.

Each year the Swift River Valley Historical Society leads a bus pilgrimage to the Prescott Peninsula, which is normally closed to the public. Recently, I was fortunate enough to make the trip. It's wonderful to see a place few contemporaries have seen, and as our bus lurched down the rutted lane, our guides, Marty Howe and Lois Barnes, pointed out the notable sites. About a mile from Gate 17, Atkinson Tavern was situated by the side of the road; and Lois also pointed out the road to the poor farm, the site of the Grange Hall, a foundation for the blacksmith shop, and a small stone bridge. Several large hills grace the peninsula, and brooks such as Prescott Brook and Egypt Brook flow southward.

The road is surrounded by thick woods, with delicate ferns growing in the understory. The occasional stone wall is the only sign that this was once a farm community. A few miles down the road, the woods open to a clearing with a modern domed structure arching high and looking rather out of place. This is the Five College Observatory, used primarily for research relating to radio signals. The observatory is situated where the center of Prescott, called Prescott Hill Village, was formerly located. This site was chosen as an observatory because of the lack of light pollution.

Farther down the lane is the former location of Conkey Tavern. The tavern was still standing until 1910 when it collapsed. Historians debate whether the exact site is now under the waters of the Quabbin or near its shoreline. A stone piece from the fireplace with the name Conkey carved into it was taken to England. Daniel Shays met fellow farmers at this tavern prior to the rebellion named for him. The rebellion occurred shortly after the American Revolution, when ordinary citizens were being taxed so heavily that they were loosing their farms to debt. Farmers were especially distressed, and Daniel Shays, a captain in the Revolutionary War, led other distraught Massachusetts farmers in a revolt against the system that was slowly crushing them financially. After Shays was driven from the grounds of the Springfield Armory, part of his army returned and camped near Prescott Center and the other part stayed at Pelham Hill. Daniel Shays' home was located half a mile east of Conkey Tavern.

South of Prescott Center is the former town of Enfield. Here the terrain becomes more rugged, with boulders dotting the woods and exposed ledges of rock rising above the vegetation. Small sections of woods where red pines had been planted have recently been logged. The road comes to an abrupt end at the edge of the reservoir. Directly across the reservoir, one can see the Enfield Lookout; and while I was there with the Swift River Valley Historical Society, I thought how strange it must have been for people using binoculars at the look-out, to see a bus pull out of the woods across the reservoir!

At the reservoir, we were able to stroll along the water's edge through what had been the outskirts of Enfield center. Bricks can still be seen at the old Parson's homestead, now tumbling into the water, and beyond lies the terraced hillside that was once the cemetery. Granite fence posts are still here, virtually all that remain of an entire village. Adjacent to one fence post is a small tree growing directly through the cracked opening of an old enamel pail. Soon the pail will split and rust away, the bricks will break apart, and only the granite fence posts will mark the place where a town once stood.

Recollections of Prescott

Ray Whitaker's family farm was located on the New Salem/Prescott line, with the barns on the Prescott side and the farmhouse across the street in New Salem. Ray was born in 1924 and was twelve years old when the Commission decided that the entire farm should be taken to protect the watershed.

"Five generations of my family," said Ray, "had lived on this land. The house that I grew up in was relatively new, because the original home was destroyed by fire in 1919. My dad rebuilt from scratch, using trees cut from the farm. Most of the lumber was chestnut. When we learned that the state would be taking our farm, we tried to disassemble the house, but the chestnut wood splintered when we tried to extract the nails. There was only one small L-section that we were able to detach from the rest of the house intact. This was sold to another family in New Salem and attached to their house.

"I think the thing that was most difficult for my father was that he had to give up the farmhouse which he had built with his own hands just a few years earlier. After the MDC bought the farm my Dad decided to rent it back because he needed more time to find another affordable farm. Money was hard to come by during the Depression. We sold our milk for 12 cents, delivered.

"Although Prescott was one of the first towns to 'surrender,' we stayed on until 1938. My parents finally found another farm in Winchendon, which I still work today. While my father was bitter about the move, I was just a kid, and I looked forward to going to a bigger high school with a real football team.

"Over the years I've taken some walks back to the old homestead. You can't see the foundation because it was cement and filled by the MDC. Beavers have made a dam flooding part of our fields. I like going back, though. At least now it's preserved for wildlife and that's a great thing."

* * *

This charcoal kiln was located in Prescott. The Commission actually began running Prescott's affairs in 1928 because many residents had sold their land to the Commission in prior years.

Lois Barnes grew up in both Prescott and Greenwich, and has vivid memories of the destruction of her towns:

"There's two things that people today overlook about the creation of the Quabbin. The first is that the process took ten years, and the towns died slowly. The second is that this all occurred during the Great Depression, so there were two crises the locals had to deal with. Not only did residents lose their homes and businesses, but the overall economy was in shambles. If you owned a business you were compensated for the land and buildings but not for the loss of the business. People were desperate. Many folks stayed in the valley to the end because they couldn't afford to move elsewhere. In fact, some people from Springfield actually moved to the four valley towns to eke out a subsistence living at dirt-cheap rents.

"As early as the year I was born [1920] there were rumors that the valley was doomed. So as long as I can remember people were moving out, and schools were consolidating. Some years there were only four or five children in school with me. Prescott was one of the first towns to be taken over by the Commission. It was like a ghost town, but Enfield was actually booming because engineers were moving into town and renting homes. My parents were the last governing officials of Prescott, and my mother used to sign the permits for the relocation of gravesites and bodies. I remember seeing workmen digging up the bones on my way to school.

"My father was very bitter about the whole thing, especially over not being paid for his business. While it was an exciting time for us kids, it was depressing for the older folks because their way of life was being taken away. People were also upset because the 3,000 'woodpeckers' who cleared the valley were from South Boston. They should have hired people from the valley to do the work, but the governor probably wanted to provide jobs for his political base. So valley folks, the ones who actually knew how to cut down a tree, were not hired, except a few who got jobs as supervisors to teach the woodpeckers. So the name 'woodpecker' is a derogatory term because valley folk thought they didn't know one end of the ax from the other.

"My family didn't leave Greenwich until September of 1938. I remember there was always smoke in the air, buildings were being bulldozed and brush was being cut and both were then torched. It was like a war zone."

Kip Waugh was only six years old when his family left Prescott, and he said that only a few memories of the town have endured over the years:

"It's interesting what you remember from such a young age, and for me it was Old Home Day down in Atkinson Hollow, which was a few miles south of our home on the north side of Prescott. I think the reason I remember those trips is because that was the only time we got ice cream other than our homemade concoctions. I can barely remember the day we left Prescott for good, but later I don't recall my father having any great bitterness. In fact, I remember him saying that our new farm in New Braintree [where Kip now operates Kip's Tree Farm] was better than the old farm. The soil in New Braintree was better because Prescott was filled with rocks and it was very hilly. As the reservoir was being built I remember that we thought the woodpeckers were a tough bunch. They would come to the square dances in New Braintree and most of them were just young guys in their early 20's. The woodpeckers were a novelty to us country kids because they all grew up in the city."

Kip offered an interesting observation as to why so many people are interested in Quabbin, and what the area might have looked like if the reservoir hadn't been built: "Years ago, nobody cared about Quabbin. It seems that it's just fairly recently that people are interested in what happened here. I think that Prescott was no different than any other poor country town, but after enough time goes by people tend to romanticize about what it was like. I often think about what this area would be like if the Quabbin hadn't been built. My guess is that many of these surrounding towns would have populations similar to a place like Shrewsbury. If the reservoir wasn't there, maybe bigger roadways would have been made and people would travel direct from Worcester toward Amherst and Northampton passing through towns like New Braintree, Hardwick, Greenwich and Prescott. The quiet towns that you see today around the reservoir would be much more developed."

This wonderful recollection from Charles Abbott first appeared in the *Athol Transcript* on April 8, 1921:

"As I am getting to be one of the oldest men in town, I think some of us old fellows should register our kick against it [the reservoir] while we can. It does not seem possible that Massachusetts would, through its legislature, even give a private corporation the right and power to destroy a number of old towns containing so many beautiful homes, many of them surrounded by noble shade trees set out by fathers, grandfathers and even great grandfathers, taking at least 150 years to bring them up to their present state of development.

> *Prescott is my home, though*
> *rough and poor she be,*
>
> *The home of many a noble soul,*
> *the birthplace of the free.*
>
> *I love her rock-bound woods and hills,*
> *they are good enough for me,*
>
> *I love her brooklets and her rills,*
> *but couldn't, wouldn't, and*
> *shouldn't love a man-made sea."*

Enfield

Enfield was originally part of Greenwich. It became its own township in 1816 and was named after one of its early settlers, Robert Field. Its principal geographic features were three hills: the Great Quabbin Mountain (now the site of the Quabbin Observation Tower), which rose five-hundred feet above the valley; Mount Ram (now at the tip of the Prescott Peninsula); and Little Quabbin Hill (now an island in the reservoir).

Enfield was also the site where the West and East Branches of the Swift River joined together just south of the town center. Because of the abundance of water power the town had a number of mills, including gristmills and fulling mills. Two of the more notable clothing mills established in Enfield in the 1800's were the Minot Manufacturing Company and the Swift River Company. A railroad connecting Athol and Springfield ran through the

Enfield boys relaxing.

Aerial view of Enfield. Mount Ram is in the center of the picture and the present-day Enfield Lookout would be in the foreground.

QUABBIN: A HISTORY AND EXPLORER'S GUIDE

center of the town, and farms were scattered throughout as the soil was of good quality.

Like Dana, Enfield had a hotel whose origins dated back to the days of the stagecoach, when travelers would rest here as the stage ran from Boston to the Berkshires. The hotel was known as the Swift River Hotel, and it operated even during the early construction of the Quabbin, hosting politicians from Boston who came out to view the project. Enfield was also the site of a home where the Commission kept its headquarters; this was the last building removed from the valley in 1940.

Enfield's center was located directly beneath the present location of the Enfield Overlook at Quabbin Park and the other village within the town, called Smith's Village or Upper Village, was just to the north. Several of Enfield's private homes were moved to Dorset, Vermont and Amherst, Massachusetts. The Enfield Methodist-Episcopal Church was moved to South Main Street in Palmer and now serves as the Grange Hall.

Enfield notables included General Joseph Hooker of Civil War fame. Hooker's grandfather, Captain Joseph Hooker, was a large landowner in town and donated the land for the Congregational Church site. His house was torn down, but the paneling, mantles, iron work, and doors were sent to New York to be incorporated into a new home.

Recollections of Enfield

In 1984, approximately 20 former residents of Dana, Prescott, Enfield, and Greenwich gathered together for a social hour. Every week since then, the faithful who grew up in the lost towns return to meet at the reservoir's Visitor Center. As the years pass, their numbers have decreased, but not their spirit — or their strong memories of life before and during the construction of the Quabbin. Many "Tuesday Tea" members are from Enfield— here are their stories.

* * *

Robert Wilder lived in Enfield as a schoolboy, and he recalls how two groups of people were affected differently by the coming of the reservoir:

"Those who worked in the mills seemed to adapt to the change a little better because they could go where the jobs were. But those who had businesses, and the farmers, had it tough. They had to start all over, and a farm can take generations to develop.

The Swift River Hotel.

"At our farm I used to sit by our old Glenwood stove and eavesdrop on my parents and grandparents. I knew the troubles they were going through, and those were trying times. When the woodpeckers and engineers came they were called the 'Boston Bastards.'

"All we got for our forty acres, barns and farmhouse was $1,500. The state didn't give us anything for the farming business we had built up over the years, just money for the land and structures. My grandfather said the timber alone on our land was worth $5,000 to $6,000. He threatened not to leave, and stayed in our house until May of 1938. He used to make moonshine in the 20's and 30's and hide it between the rows of corn.

"I'll never forget when my grandmother came home and said, 'Well, it's time to go.' On the first moving trip from our home I rode with the cows in the back of the truck. My grandfather had also packed up his still in case he needed to go back into the moonshine business. I recall that as we passed through Ware I noticed the people were dressed nicer than we were, and that was the first time I realized we were poor. Oh yes, those were trying times! We rented two different homes before finally renting a farm in Warren. Some of our old neighbors had relocated nearby, so that made it better."

* * *

Bunny Beardsley was also from Enfield. "We didn't know we were poor," says Bunny with a sly smile, "until people told us. We always had plenty to eat, mostly fresh vegetables, because meat was expensive." Bunny recalls her parents warning her not to go out after dark when the "woodpeckers from Boston came in to clear out all the trees. We understood those woodpeckers included some convicts. Some of the woodpeckers used to hide and sleep under the brush to get out of work. One day some of the kids set the fields on fire and that woke them up in a hurry! The engineers were a different matter altogether. In fact a lot of the local girls ended up marrying them."

Bunny earned extra money after school by working in the store attached to the post office. "I was there the last day the post office was open and people from all over were coming to have letters and postcards stamped with the last date stamp from Enfield."

While Bunny didn't find the forced move too difficult, her parents certainly did: "My dad was a farmer and it broke his heart. When we had moved he would often say things like, 'this food tasted better in Enfield,' or 'I wished to heck I was back in Enfield.' Once we moved he didn't last long and soon died."

THE LOST TOWNS

A home in Enfield, with the transition from horse to automobile.

* * *

Harrison Thresher grew up in Greenwich (see Greenwich overview) but was working for the Commission in Enfield when the Congregational Church caught fire in 1936:

"I was burning brush when we got the call to come fight a fire at the church, but when we got there the whole church was in flames. I watched as the steeple caught fire and the church bell fell through the church. The church had been scheduled to be demolished and it's a mystery how the fire started. Some people thought a resident of Enfield did it rather than see the church torn down."

Not all the people who remember the final days of the Swift River Valley grew up there. Some moved into the valley while others were moving out, and that's when Jim and Doris Cargill first met. "We both grew up in Springfield," remembers Jim. "Doris moved to Enfield in 1933, and I moved there in 1935 when the state was renting the empty houses.. My family had never farmed, but because it was the Depression and my dad didn't have a job, he took the opportunity to rent a 100-acre farm for $5 a month. Our family had no money, but living there was much better than Springfield since we could grow our own food. It turned out to be a blessing, especially since some families had to turn their kids over to the state because they were afraid they couldn't feed them. My mother said that the few years we lived at the farm were the happiest of her life. Doris and I met when we were ten years old. Then, when Enfield was gone, we met again when our families camped on Lake Wickaboag, and that's where the romance started. I chased her 'til she caught me. We were married in 1941, two weeks before Pearl Harbor."

Jim has one unusual recollection about going back to the abandoned homesite over thirty years later: "There was a severe drought in 1967 that lowered the reservoir. I went to where the old homestead had been and found a toy train I once owned."

* * *

The Farewell Ball of 1938 was held at the Enfield Town Hall to commemorate " the passing of the town of Enfield and Swift River Valley." Held on April 27th, the flyers for the ball read:

> Come old timers, new comers and friends of all
> for a last good time, whether you dance or not.
> Tickets: Dance $1.00, Concert .50.
> Concert 8 to 8:30, McEnelly's Orchestra - 10 piece.
> Dancing 9 to 2. Lunch at midnight.
> Electric effects by Cent. Mass. Elec. Co.

* * *

In 1938 Robert V. Johnston, an Enfield native, penned a short recollection of his days fishing the valley:

"The writer was able, and did catch his limit of trout on the opening day of the present season, nor was he the only one who did this; but without exception every native was able to secure his legal catch and do this in time to go to

Enjoying a ride at the Martindale Farm.

his daily labors at seven or eight o'clock. These trout were not the black-bellied hatchery variety, but the beautiful light-colored, brilliantly-spotted fellows of these Swift waters. From the time we were able to distinguish the fish in the Swift waters in the spring, every boy with this apparently inherited love for the woods and streams was anxious to be able to be the first to spread the word that, 'The trout were running,' and 'laying in under the dam and bridge.'

"No mention has been made of the West Branch of the Swift River whose waters, rising in the Cooleyville Hills, rapidly flow on through Rattlesnake Den, Bobbin Hollow, and on down to empty into the main branch of the Swift River near the Belchertown line. The virtues of this stream have been extolled often, and it is as well known to those Springfield fishermen who really love to fish as any other in the state; but to one who has fished this stream year in and year out, the days are easily recalled when as a boy, he accompanied his father to its banks and saw him hook a baby field mouse, all hairless and pink, through the back of the neck and toss it into what was in those days a lone, wide trout-filled hole, and immediately a great fish accepted this challenge for his supper and after a struggle was unceremoniously dumped onto the bank (without a net, of course—they were unheard of then) a fish of perhaps one-and-a-half to two pounds.

"Recollections come of the nights we went spearing; and by the flare of a large pine knot, dripping with pitch, the fish—in this case usually a sucker—would be seen lazily hugging the bottom of the stream. The spear was poised and driven at its mark. Then came the death struggle, and when all was still, he was lifted to the bank or boat and put in a burlap bag. After enough were secured, which usually meant enough to go around to make a liberal distribution to the neighbors, the horse was headed homeward."

Enfield Train Station. The "Rabbit Train" ran through Enfield and the valley connecting Springfield to Athol.

THE LOST TOWNS

Panoramic view of Enfield in 1878, a similar view can be seen today from the Enfield Lookout.

Greenwich

Ironically, the town of Greenwich, originally established in 1739, was initially called Quabbin. In 1749 it was incorporated as Quabbin Parish, and in 1754 it became a township named Greenwich after the British Duke of Greenwich.

Greenwich was located along the East and Middle branches of the Swift River in what is now the central portion of the reservoir. The terrain of the town was generally flat except for Curtis Hill, Mount Liz and Mount Pomeroy, the latter two named for settlers who were said to have been killed by Indians. Like the other lost towns, Greenwich was agricultural, with a sprinkling of small manufacturing mills including sawmills. Other businesses included silver plating, carriage making, and shops that made scythes, brushes and brooms. Greenwich benefited from a branch of the Boston and Albany Railway that opened in 1871 and ran from Springfield to Athol, going through the heart of the Swift River Valley.

One of its more distinctive industries was the ice harvesting that occurred each winter on Greenwich Lake. The ice was stored in icehouses, insulated by sawdust, then transported to the cities by rail for summer use. Over 100,000 tons of ice were cut each year and shipped to New York City, New Haven and Springfield.

Because Greenwich had many lakes and ponds, the town attracted visitors who would summer at the hundreds of cottages which dotted the lake shores. Young women would enjoy the YWCA camp on Greenwich Lake. Others would stay at the Riverside Hotel in Greenwich Village (located at the northern end of the town) or the Quabbin Inn with its 100 rooms located on Quabbin Lake. A nine-hole golf course, the Dugmar Country Club, was created for the upper class. (The stonewalls of the clubhouse still stand on Curtis Island in the reservoir, the only portion of any building left standing in the Quabbin Reservation.)

Greenwich was also home to the Hillside School, established in 1901 for the purpose of educating underprivileged boys. It was originally run by Charlotte Drinkwater and Mary Warren, two sisters and residents of Greenwich. Drinkwater and Warren were concerned about the need for underprivileged

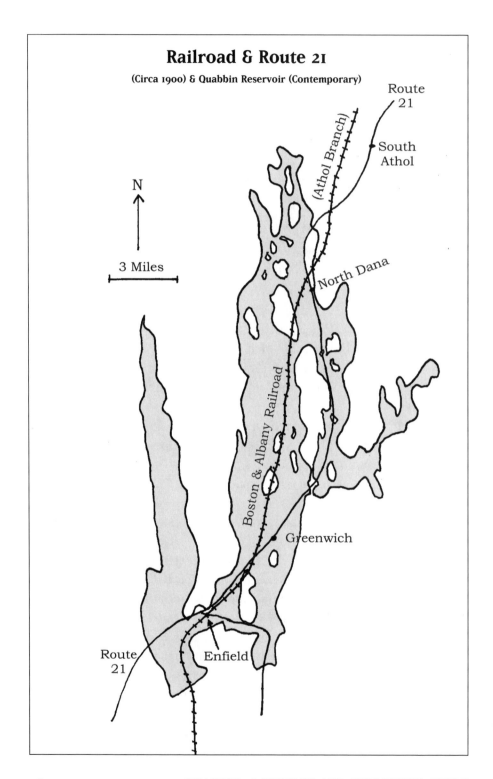

Railroad & Route 21

(Circa 1900) & Quabbin Reservoir (Contemporary)

Route
21

South
Athol

(Athol Branch)

N

3 Miles

North Dana

Boston & Albany Railroad

Greenwich

Route
21

Enfield

and orphaned children to receive an education that would prepare them to make a living. In 1938, Amy Spink and Mabel Jones wrote in *The Springfield Union* that the school graduated boys "strong in body, having learned to work intelligently, and having received moral and mental training." Besides typical studies, the boys would also "plant, cultivate, and harvest many vegetables and fruits used at the home. They also raise and store in barns, grain and hay for the horses cows, pigs, and chickens. Experts in the various lines of agriculture are supervisors of the boys, and modern methods are used at all times. The surplus products are sold, bringing in a much needed income." In 1926 the school was moved to Marlborough, Massachusetts when it was clear the valley would be flooded.

Noted artist Burt Brooks was a Greenwich native and his handsome landscapes of the valley graced many homes in the area (some presently hang in the Swift River Valley Historical Society). Brooks loved to paint the farmhouses, barns and fences of his beloved town. He even painted a scene of his country home on a wooden coffin he hoped to be buried in, taking the casket with him when he later moved to Los Angeles. Author Donald Howe relates that despite all this effort, Brooks "was finally cremated and the casket was not used." Swift River Historical Society Director Elizabeth Peirce said that Brooks' ashes were buried in Quabbin Park Cemetery but no one knows what happened to the decorative casket. "How I would love to find out what became of the casket," said Peirce.

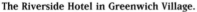

The Riverside Hotel in Greenwich Village.

Recollections of Greenwich

Harvey Dickinson was born in Greenwich and was seven years old in 1931 when his family had to leave town:

"To a kid it was all fascinating, but for the older people it was really hard. My most powerful memory of Greenwich is the wonderful swimming hole we had on the Swift River. The river curled around a bend forming a sandy beach and the water was so pure and clean. A tree hung over the pool and we used to swing from a rope and drop into the water. So many happy days! I also spent a lot of time at Quabbin Lake. My mother had a hot dog stand and rented canoes there. We would spend the summer at the lake in a cabin by the hot dog stand. Unemployed workers from the cities would hear rumors of jobs at the Quabbin and many arrived with nothing more than the shirts on their backs. My mother fed those that she could.

"My father was the post master at Greenwich Plains for 25 years until the post office closed in 1931. He also ran a general store, but by 1931 he wanted to get out because the town was dying. So we moved to Belchertown, which was a big adventure for me. I went back to Greenwich once with my uncle to see the construction progress for the reservoir, but my father didn't want to see it and he never went back. Leaving the valley really didn't sink in with me until I had my own children and realized I couldn't show them where I had grown up."

* * *

Harrison Thresher is a regular at the weekly "Tuesday Tea" held by former residents of the lost towns. Born in 1914, he grew up in Greenwich Village, where his dad was the town's mail carrier:

"My wife and I were the last couple to get married in the valley. That was June 30, 1938. We were married in my wife's parent's home in Enfield, just before the home was razed. It was great to grow up in the valley. I was one of the last ones in the North School. Toward the end, there were only six of us in the school and we were all cousins or distant cousins. I remember the surveyors would come around and flirt with the teachers. The Rabbit Train ran until 1936 so people still had good transportation. They called it the 'Rabbit' because it hopped then stopped and hopped again, making 19 stops in the 46 miles it ran from Springfield to Athol.

"I hated to leave the good times in the valley, like the square dances up in North Dana for 25 cents; but on the other hand I wanted to go to a different home with indoor plumbing, paved roads and electricity. We lived on my grandfather's 300-acre farm with no electricity, and I would have to study by those dim kerosene lights. My grandfather was really upset about having to leave his farm. Although the state paid him for his acreage, they didn't compensate him for his farming income or even for the value of the land's hardwood trees. My mother didn't want to go either, and she refused to move the first few years when others were leaving the valley. It was different for me, though. I got a job with the Metropolitan District Water Supply Commission. I worked in the nursery where the Commission raised their own trees to plant in the fields around where the reservoir would be. We used to go out and collect seeds from the white pines by banging the branches."

There were four nurseries used by the Commission that grew red spruce, white and red pine, Norway spruce, hemlock, and European larch. Millions of trees were planted to retain moisture and prevent soil erosion, as well as for their future commercial value. Planters worked in teams, one man making a hole, closely followed by a second who planted a tree generally in rows five feet apart. One planter found fifty Native-American relics during the digging.

One of Mr. Thresher's most vivid memories is the Hurricane of 1938:

"My brother and I were out walking and a woman came running out and told us a bad storm was coming. When my brother and I got home we went up in the cupola and watched the storm roll in. We saw the roof of a nearby factory rise up and down, then come flying right off. After that we got out of the cupola in a hurry! But we made good money from the storm, driving a tractor all around and clearing up trees. A house we later lived in had a piece of slate imbedded in the wall of the bathroom—it was blown right off the church and came into our house."

* * *

Betty Howe (whose father wrote Quabbin: The Lost Valley in 1951) also remembered the Hurricane of 1938.

"My boyfriend was driving me home from West Springfield's Big E [Eastern States Exposition] the day before the hurricane stuck. It was dark and pouring rain, and we got stuck near my house where a river had crossed the road. The best part was that my boyfriend had to stay over, sleeping with my brothers. Then the next day we went out to see the swollen rivers, but the wind started to pick up. A chimney came down next to us and landed on his car."

* * *

The late Clifton Peirce's story was recorded by his wife Elizabeth and related to me. Elizabeth is the one of the top Swift River Valley historians, giving tirelessly of her time to the Swift River Valley Historical Society. "I do it," she said, "in my husband's memory because I loved him so much.

"Clifton Peirce was born in 1923 in Atkinson Hollow in Prescott, the sixth

generation of his family to live there. When he was six years old his family moved to Greenwich. His father owned the general store in Atkinson Hollow and he did not want to move. But his mother felt she had no choice, because in 1929 the schools in Prescott were closing up, and she insisted he enroll in school. She told his father that if he wasn't going to leave, she would take Clifton and move without him. Eventually they resettled in Greenwich, living in Burt

THE LOST TOWNS   53

Brooks' house, the home he loved so much. His father was able to get a job with the MDC maintaining the roads and they enjoyed their time at Greenwich, even though neighbors were packing up and leaving. But in 1938 the registered letter came saying that they had to go."

The family then moved to Orange, where Clifton and Elizabeth met at the high school. "To my way of thinking," said Elizabeth, "the only good thing that came out of flooding the valley was that Clifton ended up at Orange High School, and we would not have met otherwise."

* * *

Most people started leaving the doomed towns in the early 1930's, but Mary Thomes and her family did the opposite, moving to Greenwich in 1932. Mary was a sickly child, and her doctor advised country air as a cure. Her parents followed this advice, relocating from Palmer to Greenwich in hopes of improving Mary's health.

"The move must have worked," said Mary, "I'm still alive and kicking in my upper 70's! When we moved to Greenwich, we knew we couldn't stay, but I loved it. Our home was right on the town green, next to the cemetery. My mother planted the most wonderful garden, and I remember all the fresh vegetables in the summer and the canning we did for the winter. Father was a carpenter, and he started taking on more jobs near Boston. My parents also supplemented their income by taking on boarders. We had many engineers and laborers who worked on the reservoir's construction live with us, and they were all excellent people.

"Because we stayed in Greenwich until the construction was almost complete, I had the chance to see the valley transform. I remember hollering to my mother, 'Come quick, they're going to give Mount Lizzie a haircut!' That was when they were cutting down all the trees on the lower half of the mountain, right up to the point where the surface of the reservoir would be. So they stripped the bottom of the Mount Lizzie, but since the top would be above the water line they left the trees alone up there.

"As 1938 approached and it was getting time to leave, I was mad at the people from Boston who were going to flood our valley. I remember wishing that the Boston folks would choke on their first glass of water from the Quabbin. Although I was just twelve years old when we left, it was heartbreaking. It was just so beautiful there! I was a shy child and in the small town life of Greenwich I felt content and protected. Now when I go back and see the Quabbin I feel empty."

Mary Thomes' mother, Mabel Jones, was an important chronicler of the life and death of the valley, writing many articles for local newspapers. Mary said her mother felt compelled to write "because so much was said about the valley that simply wasn't true, and my mother wanted to set the record straight." Besides Mabel's newspaper articles, she was also an accomplished poet, and her poem, "A Quabbin Neighbor," takes a sad and poignant look at Greenwich's last days:

> *Another link is broken, another neighbor gone:*
> *Another light extinguished, in this valley so forlorn.*
>
> *The homestead now abandoned, looks cold, and sad, and bare;*
> *Its windows stare like vacant eyes; there's no footsteps on the stair.*
>
> *Not by choice, dear homestead, have you been left alone,*
> *But in the March of Progress, they say your doom has come.*

Dana

Dana was incorporated in 1801 and was pieced together from sections of Petersham, Greenwich and Hardwick. It's ironic to note that when Dana was disincorporated most of its land was given back to Petersham. The town of Dana was comprised of various villages which included Storrsville, North Dana, Doubleday Village and Dana Center. North Dana was located on the middle branch of the Swift River and was a manufacturing town with several mills. Doubleday Village, home to several families of the Doubleday clan, was located between Dana Center and North Dana. Storrsville was a small village located at the eastern end of town.

Dana Center, which most people simply referred to as Dana, was the seat of the village government. Besides being known for its handsome residential area, greater Dana Center was a summer resort with many camps on nearby lakes. Unlike the other towns lost to the Quabbin, Dana Center remains above water; its town green is clearly discernable and it is kept mowed by the MDC even though it lies a mile and half into the woods at Gate 40.

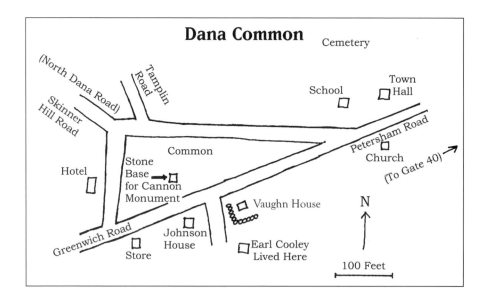

Dana Common

Cemetery

(North Dana Road)

Skinner Hill Road

Tamplin Road

School

Town Hall

Common

Petersham Road

Hotel

Stone Base for Cannon Monument

Church

(To Gate 40)

Vaughn House

N

Greenwich Road

Johnson House

Earl Cooley Lived Here

Store

100 Feet

One of the more successful businesses of the villages of Dana, particularly in the mid-1800's, was the manufacture of palm-leaf hats. The palm used to braid these hats was imported from South America. This enterprise allowed many of the women to supplement their family's income by working from their homes, where they braided the palm leaves by hand and then returned their work to the factory where finishing operations were performed. North Dana, where the factory was located, became known as "hat town." Hats from Dana were sent around the world, particularly to tropical countries where their light weight was prized. They were also popular in America in the 1860's when Shaker bonnets were in style.

Soapstone, quarried in Prescott, was brought to Dana where it was manufactured into items such as soapstone sinks. Because soapstone retains heat well, many people purchased pieces of it to heat the bottoms of their beds to keep their feet warm on winter nights. The soapstone factory was located in North Dana. After this factory was converted to a box manufacturing shop, a small generator was installed, making Dana the first town in the valley to have electricity.

Box manufacturing was a successful business and the Swift River Box Company prospered from 1890 to 1935, making boxes to house such items as apples, beverages, spices and hardware. The Athol and Enfield Railroad ran through North Dana and boxes could be transported far and wide by rail.

North Dana was also home to a counterfeit silver moneymaker in the late 1700's, according to Evelina Gustafson. In her book *Ghost Towns Beneath Quabbin*, published in 1940, she writes that the home of counterfeiter Glazier Wheeler stood near the railroad in North Dana. Apparently Wheeler hid his equipment and collection by the Swift River in a cave that he could reach by boat. He used a hollow tree as a chimney, which proved to be his downfall when raccoon hunters saw smoke coming from the tree and investigated.

There were several churches in Dana, and some church bells were used to convey important information such as local deaths. Nine rings meant a man had died, five rings a woman, and three a child. The church bell from the Congregational Church in Dana Center was moved to the United Pentacostal Church in Worcester.

Dana's population from the 1800's to 1920 stayed below the 1,000 mark, peaking near the turn of the century at about 800 residents. Greenwich and Prescott had slightly lower populations, and Enfield had the most residents with figures ranging from approximately 800 to 1,100 between the beginning of the 1800's to 1920.

Dana Common looking south at the Stevens Store on the right and Johnson House on the left.

QUABBIN: A HISTORY AND EXPLORER'S GUIDE

Recollections of Dana

The elderly folks sit in lawn chairs deep in the woods at the edge of a sunny clearing. They are shaded by sprawling sugar maples and surrounded by scattered stone foundations and a handful of dirt roads. Laughter echoes through the trees as someone recounts a story of days gone by, when the grassy clearing had been the location of the town common and handsome homes rested atop their stone foundations. The Dana Reunion is in full swing.

The Cooley Brothers, Earl and Douglas, along with their sister Florence May Avery, show me the location where their home once stood, just a few feet off a side road to the south of the green. They explain how their dad had been an auto mechanic who worked in a converted blacksmith shop. They can still remember the forge, bellows, anvil and giant sling used to lift oxen crowding the same space where their father had worked on Model T's.

"When we had to leave in the late 30's," recalled Earl, "my dad was devastated. He tried to restart his auto repair business in Petersham, but it didn't work. Eventually he ended up in a sawmill in Athol. I was 12 years old when we had to leave. For years we were not allowed to come back into Dana to see where the old house had once stood. They took away our house, our town and even the chance to revisit. But we were still here in Dana when the Hurricane of '38 hit. That was quite an experience—took us three days of work to cut and move trees off the road until we could reach where Route 32 now runs."

Earl walks over to a unique stone retaining wall featuring small rounded stones placed in cement. "This was where the Vaughn's house was. See where the stones are chipped on the corner?" Earl pauses, smiles and shakes his head. "I was going a little too fast in the buggy, and when I took this bend we hit the stones!"

Florence laughs. "I remember that! I also remember listening to Mrs. Johnson play the harp across the street. It was beautiful."

* * *

Vernon Vaughn explains that he grew up on Tamplin Road and it was his grandfather who had the house on the common with the beautiful retaining wall. "Having to leave our home really didn't hit me at the time. I was only 14 and I used to think Athol was a big city!" Vernon ambles over to the north side of the common and heads to a spot where trees grow by a field. "This is where the two-room elementary school was located. Each row of seats was a different grade, with the older kids upstairs. I started school here in 1929. The sixth, seventh and eighth-graders went to the North Dana Grammar School, then, for high school, the kids were bussed to New Salem or Petersham—there was no high school in Dana or North Dana. In 1938 I was in the eighth grade and it was the last graduating class of North Dana Grammar School. There were only three of us in the class."

* * *

Katherine O'Brien Reed lived in North Dana. "When I first heard the news about flooding the valley I thought for sure it was just a rumor," she recalled. "I couldn't seem to make it sink in. But I soon realized it was real as I watched my dad and mom get bitter. Our options were, 'you either sell or we take.' Many of the women in North Dana worked in a hat shop so it meant loosing their jobs."

* * *

Recording the memories of these people had a surreal quality for this writer. For years I'd been coming to Dana alone, wondering what the town was like when it was full of life and who the people were that called this place home. How odd it was to sit under the big maple in front of the Vaughn house listening to the very people I had wondered about. They are all in their late 70's, 80's and 90's now, but back in the 1930's they were just kids. Each had special memories very different from the others. Many of these memories were of unusual happenings that would stick in the mind of any kid. One resident recalled seeing a dead man

The Eagle Hotel on Dana Common.

QUABBIN: A HISTORY AND EXPLORER'S GUIDE

in an automobile at a place that was then named "Dead Man's Curve". Another told the story of how her mother held off an escapee from an insane asylum with a shotgun and how she would keep all the kids inside the house whenever the "Gypsies" traveled the valley.

Jean Ewing, who used to spend summers in Dana at her grandmother's, summed up this simpler time with these words: "I remember my sister and I would sit on the cannon in the middle of the green, then we would go over to the village store and look everything over. At night, if we were feeling mischievous, we would go back to the cannon and put a few firecrackers in it to make it boom. Dana was a great place for a kid."

* * *

Ernie Carrington was not able to attend the reunion and instead mailed me a story he wrote, chronicling one of his adventures on a farm in Dana in 1925 when he was seven years old. At that early age Ernie had hired himself out to look after the Johnson family cow. "Each morning," wrote Ernie, "as soon as the milking was out of the way, I snapped a lead-rope onto the cow's halter and walked her out to pasture, which was quite a long way out of town. Part of the way was by the regularly traveled road between Dana and North Dana. To get to the pasture I had to turn off from that road onto an old wagon road, which lead through the forest into an open meadow." Ernie explained that he let the cow into the pasture, and, "as the cow stepped into the open, I noticed she quickly looked to her left and shied away. I looked up and saw a big gray wolf dart out from behind some brush and then stop and turn toward me. I was quite short in those days and we were eyeball to eyeball. I don't know how long we stood there like that, and I hardly dared to breathe." Ernie finished the story by writing how he saw the muscles on the wolf relax, and then it trotted off across the field and headed into the woods.

* * *

Another interesting letter I received came from Wendy Anderson, who explained that her grandfather, Guy L. Marvel, was the last to leave Dana just after the bombing of Pearl Harbor. Wendy writes:

"Grandfather did not want to accept the offer the state gave him for his 'life.' He was a chicken farmer and also had a fish hatchery at one time. While he went through court battles with the state, the progress of the reservoir went

The Edgar Vaughn residence. The unique retaining wall in the lower right of the picture can still be seen today on the south side of Dana Common.

on around him. His friends left the area, and he was thought a fool. The Commission put up the gates, blocking the roadways, and the gate blocking the road to my grandfather's was Gate 41 off Route 32A in Petersham. For a period of time a guard was stationed there to let my grandfather and his family in and out. In the end, with no support from outside sources, he lost his battle, and sold his home to the Commission for less than they originally offered. But he didn't move far. To spite the Commission he bought the land right across the street [Route 32A] from the gate."

* * *

Elizabeth Peirce, President of the Swift River Valley Historical Society, was a good friend of former Dana resident Bill O'Brien, now deceased. Bill was a young man living in Dana when the "woodpeckers" and he relayed this story to Elizabeth:

"The woodpeckers would get drunk on Saturday night, steal cars and raise hell. One Saturday night a carful approached my brothers and me asking if we had seen a fella's arm. Seems one of the occupants had his arm out the window when the driver swerved too close to a tree. Killed the man and tore his arm right off. That place was called 'Dead Man's Curve.'"

* * *

Bertha Taylor is one of the few people that lived in all three of the lost towns—Enfield, Greenwich, and North Dana:

"The last village I lived in was Doubleday Village, which was located in North Dana, about halfway between the center of North Dana and Dana. The village got its name because at one time everybody who lived in the six houses by the crossroads was a Doubleday. I was 12 years old when we had to leave, and I really hated to go because I'd probably never see my friends again. Most of the people from town were moving to surrounding towns, but we relocated to New Hampshire.

"My memory is not as sharp as it should be but certain memories about Doubleday Village stay with me. I remember there used to be a small pond near our house, and we had a wonderful time swimming there and then picking mayflowers on the walk home. Sometimes when I was walking to school, Mr. Cooley [Earl's father] would stop and give me a ride, and he always called me "Little Bill" because I looked just like my dad. My father was the iceman, and he peddled ice to all the nearby towns and always seemed to be on the road.

"Doubleday Village was a wonderful place to grow up if you liked the country life. I went back there years ago, and I had a hard time finding where our house had been because it was all woods. But since our house was on a little ridge, I was eventually able to locate its foundation."

A Tour of Dana With Former Resident Earl Cooley

Former resident of Dana, Earl Cooley, recently gave me a tour of some of his favorite places near the Dana town common. He had been given a special permit to drive his truck on the Gate 40 access road which leads into the common.

"The people who lived here," said Earl, "just couldn't believe their houses were being taken away from them and that they had no say about it. Some folks tried to fight it, like Mr. Johnson, a judge whose home was right on the common. He took the Commission to court but it didn't do him a bit of good."

The first area Earl showed me was the site where local eccentric "Popcorn" Snow had been buried. Snow had a metal casket designed for himself that featured a glass panel built into the lid above the area where his head would lay.

Dana Town Hall, with the cemetery behind it. The walkway to the town hall can still be seen today on the northeast side of Dana Common.

He feared being buried alive and instructed his wife that upon his death she appoint someone to look through the glass panel for seven days after his burial to make sure he was dead! He died in 1872 and his casket was placed in a tomb located in the cemetery just beyond Gate 40. Earl commented that after the MDC moved all the graves, "They filled in Snow's tomb, but I could never understand why. I considered it a piece of history."

I asked Earl if Popcorn Snow's wishes were followed after his death. "Partially," said Earl. "My father said that the undertaker looked in on Snow for three days after his death. Later, the door to the tomb was open, and when my father was a kid, he and the other boys would dare each other to go in with a flashlight to peek at Popcorn's face. He told me he did that a few times!"[1]

After visiting the site of Snow's tomb, Earl and I drove down the main road to Dana common. Earl pointed out a couple of small streams, explaining how he would catch small brook trout in them as a child. We passed a little shack on the right which is currently used as a deer checking station, and on the same side of

1 The cemetery where Snow's tomb was located, like all the others inside the reservation, was removed and the bodies reinterred, most of which were placed in the Quabbin Park Cemetery. The exact location of Popcorn Snow's tomb can be reached by walking beyond Gate 40 on the main road to Dana common for about 200 feet then turning right on a dirt road and following that for another 100 to 150 feet.

QUABBIN: A HISTORY AND EXPLORER'S GUIDE

the road is a large stonewall which was once part of a barn for the town's poor farm which operated in the late 1800's through the early 1900's. People at the poor farm would work for room and board. "These were folks from the area that hit hard times or had no family," said Earl. "This was long before there was a welfare system. We never had any problems with the people that lived and worked there. We considered them part of the town. One reason I remember the farm so well is because it was my job to walk my grandfather's cow to the town farm whenever the cow was in heat so the bull could service it."

About a mile down the main road to Dana common is an old road on the left-hand side that was known as the Barre-Dana Road which headed southeast over the East Branch of the Swift River toward Barre. The bridge over the river is no longer there, and much of the road is overgrown.

Earl and I continued a short way toward Dana common and he pointed out a turn-off to the right that parallels the main road a short distance and then reconnects with it. This was the original road to Dana before it was straightened to avoid the sharp curve. "The school teachers boarded at one of the homes along the turn-off," said Earl.

A view of Dana Common looking toward the northeast. From left to right on the picture: The Eagle Hotel, the Flagg residence, elementary school, and the town hall.

About 75 feet from the spot where the parallel road reconnects with the main road is the former site of the blacksmith's residence. Here, a stone rests on top of another on the left-hand side of the road, and on the top stone there is a bolt. Chiseled in the stone is the date "1899." This marks where Moses Marcille lived until a fire destroyed his home in 1899. (Marcille later moved closer to Dana common where he shot himself after first wounding his wife.)

Through the trees to the left of the main road, we glimpsed Pottapaug Pond which is fed by the East Branch of the Swift River. Pottapaug runs south to the boat launch at Gate 43 where the pond connects with the Quabbin. Earl explained that Pottapaug had been much smaller when he lived in Dana, and was expanded in size by the dam by the boat launch.

As we approached the common, the road forks at a granite memorial marker. Earl and I parked his truck and walked ahead while he explained the significance of cellar holes, walkways, granite posts, and stone foundations. The following description takes you in a counter-clockwise direction, starting with the former location of the town hall to the right, just before the fork in the road. The cement walkway that led to the town hall's front door is still visible. (Earl explained that the town hall building had been a church prior to its purchase by the town, and visitors to Dana were often confused because the active church was located across the street.) The town's school was located next to the town hall (a cellar hole is still visible here) and behind both buildings was the Dana Center Cemetery. The granite posts which once supported the fence bordering the cemetery are still standing. Next to the school was the Flagg home, one of the larger homes on the common. The next dirt road on the right is Tamplin Road, which runs to the north where more homes were once clustered. Just beyond Tamplin Road is a paved road heading northwest. This was called Skinner Hill Road/North Dana Road; it led to Skinner Hill, passed Dead Man's Curve, and went on to North Dana prior to the construction of the reservoir.

A cannon once stood at the east end of the common. Its cement base is still visible, but the cannon has been relocated to the Quabbin Park Cemetery. Nearby, a basswood tree which flowers in July provides shade. It can be identified by its large leaves which, at the base, are unequally heart-shaped and have tiny teeth on their margins. On the west end of the common was an iron water trough fed from a spring just to the north.

Directly west of the common was the Eagle Hotel, and its cellar hole is still visible. The two-story hotel had a handsome porch facing the common and four white columns on its front side, facing south. As we continued our loop of the common we passed a paved roadway heading to the southeast called Greenwich Road. Earl and I walked to the southeastern side of the common where the general store and post office were located; their concrete foundations can still be seen. The next large cellar hole and retaining wall belonged to the Johnson residence, one of the larger homes on the common. Earl explained that Mrs. Johnson played the harp in the afternoons and "us kids would stand on the retaining wall and listen to that wonderful music. When Mrs. Johnson was finished she would say 'come on in' and we'd all have milk and cookies."

Next to the Johnson house a dirt road heads to the south. There is a sugar maple here with a hollow opening, large enough for a person to stand in. (This tree will probably only survive a few more years because it is decaying.) Next to the hollow tree is another large sugar maple which children love to climb. Located on the east side of this dirt road was the Vaughn house, whose front doorway looked out onto the main road and the common. A unique retaining wall made from smooth stones runs along the side and back of the house site. Earl's home was next to the Vaughn house, just a few feet south on the dirt road. The Congregational Church stood to the east of the Vaughn house on the main road, opposite the town hall.

* * *

Most of the businesses in the area were located in North Dana, which is now under water. Earl and I took a drive toward North Dana on North Dana Road, heading by Skinner Hill and passing Dead Man's Curve. There were many accidents here and it's easy to imagine how difficult negotiating this curve would have been at night. North Dana Road abruptly ends about two miles from Dana common at the shore of the Quabbin. This area is known as Graves Landing; here Warden Franklin Graves had a boat landing from which he patrolled Quabbin. (There is a memorial stone marker on the right.)

We then returned to the common and followed Greenwich Road for approximately a mile and a quarter to an overgrown dirt road on the left. From here we walked up the dirt road to a side trail on the left that leads to an old plane wreck in the middle of the forest.[2] Twisted hunks of steel and a four-foot crater created by the plane's impact were all that remained. We estimated the plane crashed sometime in the 1950's from the way the trees had grown up around it. (I later learned from historian Joe Cernauskas that our estimate was on target. Joe explained that this was the site where a military jet (F-94C) crashed in the late 1950's. The pilot was able to eject and landed safely on Mount Zion.)

Earl also showed me a special boyhood place hidden in the woods called the "Indian Kitchen." Legend says that Native Americans used it for shelter and cooking. The Indian Kitchen is a natural rock shelter with a granite overhang of rock about 12 feet off the ground that protects an area about seven feet wide and 55 feet long. Inside this cave-like shelter is a formation that Earl refers to as the "oven"—a perfectly shaped, 2 foot by 2 foot hole in the granite ideal for bak-

---

2 Directions to plane crash site: From the Dana common it's a mile and a quarter to the dirt road on the left just after a small white pine field (or 6/10 of a mile past a big swamp). Follow the dirt road. The first cut-off trail on the left leads to the plane.

Harvey's Inn in North Dana.

QUABBIN: A HISTORY AND EXPLORER'S GUIDE

ing. This shelter is halfway up a cliff and from this lofty perch you can look down through the trees to the southeast. Native Americans would have certainly known about and used a shelter like this. It would have been possible to stay out of the wind, rain and snow, as they did at the Rock House Reservation in West Brookfield.

As we arrived at the Indian Kitchen it started to rain, but we stayed dry, sitting on boulders inside the shelter, talking of the days when Earl would come here from his Dana home for picnics. "We used to leave a glass jar, pencil and paper here where people would leave their name and the date they visited," said Earl. "So a few years ago I brought a new jar to start the practice again." He showed me the jar with a few names written in it, tucked away by the oven.

Animals had also used the shelter recently. At its northern end was a pile of droppings that resembled those of a mountain lion. I asked Earl if he believed mountain lions lived at Quabbin and he said, "Yes, I think it's possible. In fact, my son said he saw the tracks of one with a long tail mark in the snow when he was logging in Hardwick along Route 32A. There are plenty of deer for them to eat, and porcupine as well. Just on the other side of this hill where there are more hemlocks, you can find many porcupine denning areas."

And so we sat there talking and watching the rain fall, probably much the same way the Native Americans had done before us.

Earl Cooley rests at the Indian Kitchen in Dana.

A Visit to the Swift River Valley
Historical Society Museum

Many people who visit the Quabbin Reservoir think that the only historic material about the lost towns on public display is the exhibit at the Quabbin Visitor Center. Just a few miles north, however, is the Swift River Valley Historical Society Museum, where every imaginable item from the valley is available for viewing. The goals of the society are to preserve materials from the towns of the Swift River Valley and to make records, memorabilia and genealogy available for research.

The museum, located in North New Salem, is housed in a cluster of buildings including the Whitaker house, a large colonial home built in 1816, and a second building that was originally the Methodist Episcopal Church built in 1837 in North Prescott near Gate 20. During the construction of the Quabbin this church was moved to Orange and again moved in 1984 to its current location. The adjacent carriage shed, which houses farm and household items as well as a replica of a one-room school, is a more recent structure, built in 1991. Also in the carriage shed is a wooden washing machine, the original fire truck from Dana, and a Native-American dugout canoe found at the bottom of Morton Pond in Enfield. The carriage shed was named the Peirce Memorial Carriage Shed in honor of Clifton Peirce who negotiated its construction during his tenure as Historical Society president.

It would be difficult to describe the many period pieces of furniture, paintings, maps and other historical memorabilia at the museum, but there are a few items that deserve special mention. On the museum grounds, visitors can't miss the odd-looking multi-sided sign board, which points the way to former locations of some of the extinct towns. This sign board was made in 1850 and once stood on Main Street in New Salem. (If you look closely at the town names you will notice that all are from the local area except one, Indianapolis, Indiana. When the sign board was being painted a former resident of New Salem asked that his new town be added.) Also outside is a "his and her" outhouse which were originally from the Morse Village School which had been located in a section of New Salem that was claimed by the state because if fell within the area of the reservation.

Inside the Whitaker House a large-scale relief map of the valley shows where homes, roads and schools were located prior to the construction of the Quabbin. (The only partially standing structure today, is the stone exterior of the Dugmore Golf Course clubhouse situated on an island in the reservoir near Gate 43.) Another unique display is the wedding dresses of the three Paige sisters from New Salem. As young girls they had made a promise that they would not wed until they could be married at the same time. This promise was kept, and all three were married in a joint ceremony in 1906, which the Boston Post referred to as "Cupid's Triple Victory."

Each of the lost towns has its own room for displaying local memorabilia in the Whitaker House. In the Greenwich room there is an interesting exhibit about Burt Brooks, a well-known painter and photographer born in Greenwich in 1849. Several of his paintings of the valley adorn the exhibit's walls. Also featured is the story of how he built his own coffin on which he painted pictures of his home. As noted in the chapter on Greenwich, Brooks moved to Los Angeles; and although he took his coffin with him, he was never buried in it.

Allow yourself at least two hours to peruse the museum, but don't be surprised if you stay twice as long. The Historical Society is a volunteer organization with an unpaid staff, and memorial gifts and bequests are welcomed. They do not buy or sell their collection.

If You Go

The Swift River Valley Historical Society Museum is located off Route 202 at 40 Elm Street in North New Salem. Membership in the Society is only $5.00 annually. Members do not pay an entrance fee to the museum and receive a quarterly newsletter, as well as a calendar of upcoming events. A genealogy collection is housed downstairs in the Prescott Church Museum.

The museum is only open at limited times: mid-June through August on Wednesdays and Sundays, 1pm-4pm; and from September through Columbus Day on Sundays only. Telephone: 978-544-6882. Mail Address: PO Box 22, New Salem, MA 01355.

THE PAST, PART III
Forgotten History of the Region

Nipmuck Warriors
and the Siege of Brookfield

King Philip's War was fought between Native Americans and Colonial settlers in 1675 and 1676. This was America's first major war, and on a per capita basis there were more casualties in this conflict than any other war in the country's history. The war began when warriors from the Wampanoag tribe and soldiers from the Plymouth and Massachusetts Bay colonies engaged in a series of skirmishes in the area that would eventually become southeastern Massachusetts, as well as the locale around the future site of Bristol, Rhode Island. Metacom, also known as King Philip, was the Wampanoag Sachem who led his warriors in a series of raids and ambushes against the colonists along the Massachusetts/Rhode Island border. Metacom subsequently moved his people out of the region and into modern-day central Massachusetts. There, the Wampanoags joined with the Nipmucks ("Fresh Water People") who had attacked Mendon, Massachusetts where they killed six colonists and put a number of homes to the torch. The leader of this raid, Matoonas, had been patiently waiting to seek revenge against the colonists. Four years earlier his son had been wrongfully accused of murdering a settler and was executed, his head stuck on a pole and displayed by English authorities to serve as a warning to other Indians.

After Mendon was attacked, colonial leaders in Boston sought damage control by trying to meet with another powerful Nipmuck leader, Muttawmp, who resided at Wenimisset near the modern day location of Brookfield, Massachusetts. In *Soldiers of King Philip's War* (written in 1891) author George M. Bodge records that the English thought it wise to locate Muttawmp immediately by sending a large party of soldiers with "more show of power to compel them to some sort of treaty." At the time, Brookfield was the only English settlement in the wilderness of central Massachusetts, and Captain Hutchinson and Captain Wheeler arrived there on July 31, 1675 with thirty troops and three Christian Indian guides. A meeting was quickly arranged between the English captains and Muttawmp for the next morning on a plain about three miles outside the town. The events that soon transpired were among the most harrowing

An engraving on Foster Hill Road shows Nipmuck warriors pushing a burning wagon of hay toward the garrison.

and dramatic of the war. History may best be understood through the power of one's imagination. Let's imagine what it may have been like to be in central Massachusetts more than three centuries ago:

* * *

Picture yourself as one of the booted and helmeted soldiers, riding your horse with the other thirty men under the command of Wheeler and Hutchinson. Christian Indian guides lead your company to the rendezvous place, but the Nipmucks are nowhere to be found. You dismount and watch the guides carefully examining the trail ahead. They shake their heads ominously, then walk to Hutchinson and warn him that many Indians have recently passed this way. The captain confers with some of the local Brookfield men who have accompanied the soldiers, and together they decide to push on and locate the Nipmucks. Having lived peacefully with the Nipmucks for years, the locals believe productive negotiations are possible.

You swear under your breath, sweat stinging your eyes under the hot August sun. Instinct tells you not to go forward, and your stomach tightens as the Christian Indians try again to warn the captain to turn back. But Hutchinson rises in his stirrups and waves his arm to go forward. You look at your comrades and their faces show the strain—they know the nearest reinforcements are many miles away in Springfield to the west, or Lancaster to the east. Still, all of you spur your horses onward; orders are orders.

You ride for another mile. There are no signs of Indians, and you begin to think they have left the region entirely. Now the trail narrows: on the left is a swamp and to the right is a steep rocky hill. You can't help but think, "Ambush!", but the long column of troopers makes its way along the trail, and you begin to relax. Then the woods explode.

A terrible volley of musket balls pours from the swamp and the hillside. Eight men fall from their horses, blood spewing from gaping wounds. You pull on the reins, turning your horse to flee, but the rear is full of charging Indians, their bloodcurdling war cries making you sick with fear. Blue-gray smoke from the Indian muskets clouds the air, and it's difficult to see Hutchinson or Wheeler. No one seems in charge.

Suddenly your horse screams, staggers and goes down. You jump off before the beast crushes you and begin running up the rock slope, arrows whizzing by. You've got your musket, but there is no time to load; several Nipmucks are right on your heels. Other troopers are already dashing ahead of you, and behind are the screams of your fallen comrades. To your left you see Wheeler fall from his saddle, and an Indian rushes to finish him off. But Wheeler's son shoots the Indian and drags his father onto his horse.

All appears lost when one of the Christian Indians signals for you to turn into a beech grove. At first you hesitate, thinking it's the opposite direction from Brookfield, but then follow, putting your life in his hands. Other soldiers are also running after the Christian Indian, and soon the war whoops of the enemy fade. You have made the right choice. The trail swings back toward Brookfield, and after a grueling march you arrive at the town.

The settlers are stunned but quickly recover, helping you and the other survivors in an effort to fortify Ayer's Tavern as a garrison. No sooner have all the town's inhabitants joined you in the tavern, than two-hundred Nipmucks set siege, firing so many musket balls it sounds like hail hitting the walls. A women falls, then a child; blood is everywhere. You fire your musket out the garret window and wound an Indian rushing the house with a torch.

There is a lull in the fighting, and you wonder if the Indians have pulled back. One foolhardy young man ventures outside to get more gunpowder from his home. But you watch from the window as two braves run him down, splitting his head open with a tomahawk. Then they hack off his head, tossing it around like a ball before impaling it on a pole.

As darkness falls, the Nipmucks tighten their noose around the house, screaming out years of seething hatred. Nearby barns and homes are put to the torch, and soon the entire village goes up in smoke. Caught up in their own rage, the Nipmucks recklessly expose themselves. Using the moonlight, you are able to shoot one of them. At three o'clock in the morning your stomach sinks as you watch the Indians gather dry, combustible hay, then send flaming arrows toward you. One lands on top of the house, and within seconds acrid smoke is seeping into the garrison. Furiously, you hack a hole in the roof and douse the burning shingles, but wonder how long the garrison will hold. Water is almost gone.

During the dawn hours you walk through the house. The dead and wounded are in one room, and among them are Hutchinson and Wheeler. Hutchinson has a gray look about him, and you fear he has not long to live, but Wheeler continues to bark out orders. In another room the women and children are huddled; one woman appears to have gone mad. Throughout the day the Indians shoot anytime a head appears at a window, and slowly the garrison's manpower is sapped.

When the sun goes down a second time, the situation is so desperate it is decided to risk sending a messenger out for help, or all will certainly parish. Ephraim Curtis, a hunter and trapper, shows great bravery and volunteers. But before he gets twenty rods from the house he's discovered and barely makes it back alive. Later, he tries again and is not heard from—no one knows if he made it or not. Now the Nipmucks charge the house and succeed in placing hay at one corner which they set afire. You know that if the licking flames take hold of the house's shingles it means death, so you and two others charge out with pails of water and douse the flames. A searing hot pain shoots through your arm— you've been hit! Somehow you manage to get back inside before losing consciousness.

When you awaken, hours have passed. You, along with the other wounded, are begging for water, but every drop is gone. The Indians seem to know this, and now they have a cart piled high with burning hay and are pushing it toward the house. Settlers shoot at the cart but the Indians are protected behind it, and all hope seems lost. The choice is awful: to stay inside means being burned alive, to run outside means being scalped by the enraged Nipmucks.

Two things happen that save your life. First, a sudden downpour extinguishes the burning wagon, and then Major Willard and his troops from Lancaster burst upon the scene. The fresh soldiers surprise the Indians and a battle ensues. Finally, the Indians reluctantly withdraw to their village at Wenimisset.

* * *

Visiting the Greater Quabbin Area Sites of King Philip's War

• Wenimesset was located along the Ware River in the present location of New Braintree on Ravine Road. Next to a tree, there is granite marker post on the north side of the road that indicates the Indian village/Metacom's Camp.

• Ayer's Garrison (also known as the Brookfield Garrison) is on Foster Hill Road, which runs parallel to Route 9 at the border of Brookfield and West Brookfield. There is a marker for John Ayers, another for the garrison, and a third marking the stone well where Major Wilson was shot. (Historian Robert Wilder points out that Major Wilson was actually Private Wilson, and the monument is in error.) Farther to the northwest there is a marker at the site of the first meeting house which was burned during the attack.

• A state marker on Route 9 near the border of Brookfield and West Brookfield describes the battle, stating, "...one garrison house was defended to the last."

• The exact site of the ambush has been debated. There is a stone marker on West Road, three-tenths of a mile north of Unitas Road that reads, "Somewhere Within 1/2 Mile Along The Base Of This Hill Capt. Edward Hutchinson And His Company Were Attacked By Indians Lying In Ambush Aug. 2, 1675 And He And More Than One Half His Men Slain Or Wounded." There is also a state marker on Route 67 in New Braintree that indicates the general area as the ambush site, referring to it as "Wheeler's Surprise."

• In the cemetery at Lake Wickaboag, a monument commemorates seven soldiers killed in the ambush who are buried here.

• My favorite historical marker in the area does not commemorate the Brookfield ambush and siege, but rather concerns English captive Mary Rowlandson and her daughter, who were taken prisoner after a native raid on the town of Lancaster. While Mary survived the ordeal and went on to write a fascinating account of her captivity, her daughter, Sarah, died after a few days of captivity from wounds suffered during the attack. A stone marker indicating the vicinity of her death and burial can be found on Thompson Road/Hardwick Road in New Braintree. The marker is difficult to see, as it is set back along a stonewall on the north side of the road. Thompson Road runs northwest off Route 67, and the marker is a little farther northwest where Hardwick Road intersects with Thompson Road. The marker reads, "Sarah P. Rowlandson, Born Sept. 5, 1669. Shot by Indians at Lancaster, Feb 10, 1676. Taken to Winnimissett Camp. Died Feb. 18, 1676."

• Significant portions of the *Narrative of Mrs. Mary Rowlandson* and *Captain Thomas Wheeler's Narrative* are included in *King Philip's War: The History and Legacy of America's Forgotten Conflict* by Eric Schultz and Michael Tougias. The book also includes a detailed history of the ambush of Wheeler and Hutchinson, and the subsequent attack on Brookfield.

The Case of the
Poison Oyster Epitaph

When I was interviewing former Prescott residents, there was one person in particular, Warren Gibbs, I would have loved to question. Warren, however, lies buried in a small windswept cemetery in Pelham.

If I could communicate with Warren, I'd ask him about his relationship with his wife and the details of his death. Now, this may seem like a strange line of questioning, but Warren's tombstone is even stranger. The weathered marble slab reveals the following epitaph:

Warren Gibbs
Died by Arsenic Poison
March 23, 1860
Age 36 years 5 mos. 23 days

Think my friends when this you see
How my wife hath dealt by me
She in some oysters did prepare
Some poison for my lot and share
Then of the same I did partake
And nature yielded to its fate
Before she my wife became
Mary Felton was her name

Erected by his brother
Wm Gibbs

A 1906 article written in the *Daily Hampshire Gazette* chronicles how Warren was seized with a burning fever in the spring of 1860: "Tortured by a burning thirst, he implored some sort of relief. A kind neighbor brought a jug of hard cider, which was almost at the vinegar stage, and the sufferer gulped down a large quantity of the liquid. The acid relieved the man's distress and he began to recover. Then his wife prepared a meal of oysters, of which he ate greedily, and soon the wretched thirst returned and the man rapidly grew worse." Gibbs died a day or two later.

Legend has it that Warren Gibbs' brother William suspected Gibbs' wife Mary of mixing arsenic in the oyster stew she cooked, but did not have enough evidence to convince authorities to perform an autopsy. Consequently, no formal criminal charges were ever brought against Mrs. Gibbs. William, however, would not let the issue drop and decided to publicly accuse Mary by way of the tombstone.

Of course, Mary and her family members were outraged by the inscription; late one night Mary's brother visited the cemetery and tipped over the stone that cast his sister as a murderer. The next day William Gibbs straightened the stone and issued a warning that if the stone was tipped again he would seek court action against his brother's wife. William also introduced an element of the supernatural, claiming that terrible things would befall anyone who desecrated the stone, and they would be cursed for life. The tipping stopped, and the stone stood unmolested for years.

The story of the "poison oyster" gravestone has prompted much interest over the years, with newspaper articles occasionally questioning the guilt and motives of Mrs. Gibbs. But Robert Lord Keyes, curator of the Pelham Historical Society, recently explained that while the gravestone is indeed a curiosity, it may also be a hoax. "Warren Gibbs' name is not on the town census," he said. "Nor have we found a death record. That makes us question the story and wonder if someone back in the 1800's had this gravestone made as a hoax. On the other hand, we do know Warren was born in 1823 in Prescott, and that Mary was also born there in 1827. We were also able to establish that Mary died on January 24, 1902 and is buried in Dwight Cemetery in Belchertown."

Keyes summarized the Gibbs' Poison Oyster Stone by saying, "This episode will probably remain a mystery. It's possible Warren Gibbs didn't live in Pelham very long and died elsewhere but was buried here. But I think it's odd no one ever produced a newspaper clipping written at the time of his death in light of his brother's accusations."

The tombstone at Gibbs' grave (located at Knights Cemetery on Packardville Road, opposite Gate 8 on Route 202) is actually a replica of the original, which resides in the Pelham Historical Society Museum. The headstone was moved to the museum in 1971 for safekeeping because of previous thefts of the stone. Robert Keyes explained that it's possible that the headstone in the museum might also be a replica, because on five different occasions in the past the stone had been stolen from the cemetery. Folklore says that each time the headstone was stolen it was recovered, perhaps because the perpetrators had second thoughts about incurring the alleged curse of William Gibbs.

One past theft resulted in the stone disappearing for a period of seven years. It was eventually recovered in 1947 when a Professor Valentine of Springfield College bought a farm in Palmer. Unaware that the tombstone had been stolen, Valentine discovered it buried in the dirt floor of his farmhouse basement. Fearing there might be a body buried beneath it, Valentine called the state police, one of whom immediately recognized the stone as the missing Gibbs gravestone from Knight's Cemetery.

Visiting the Poison Oyster Headstone
and the Pelham Historical Society Museum

Knight's cemetery is located one-tenth of a mile down Packardville Road, opposite Gate 8 on Route 202. The Gibbs stone is at the front of the cemetery in the far right corner as you face the cemetery.

The Pelham Historical Society Museum is located at the corner of Route 202 and Amherst Road in Pelham. The museum is housed in the former Congregational Church, circa 1839, which was abandoned as a parish in 1936 when its members dispersed because of the building of the Quabbin. The museum is open from June 1st through September 30th on Sundays from 1pm to 4pm.

Her Husband Is in the Well
(A Strange Tale of Murder)

In 1778 in rural Brookfield, a desperate woman by the name of Bathesheba Spooner decided that the solution to her many problems was to have her husband murdered. The events that followed were soon labeled by local newspapers as the most extraordinary crime ever perpetrated in New England.[1]

This bizarre tale begins when a Continental soldier, just 16 years old, passed through Brookfield on his way home after fighting under the command of General George Washington. The boy's name was Ezra Ross, and he was ill and hungry, having walked all the way from New Jersey. Bathesheba Spooner must have taken pity on the boy as he staggered by her home, because she took him in and nursed him back to health.

Although Bathesheba was married at the time to 37-year-old Joshua Spooner, it was an unhappy union, and she told friends she had developed an "utter aversion" to her husband. It was reported he was "an abusive drunkard" and acted in a "cowardly, unmanly way." Apparently, the young Ezra Ross stood in stark contrast to Mr. Spooner, and Bathesheba and Ross became close during his recuperation at her home. So close, in fact, that they became lovers and Bathesheba became pregnant by him.

Because of her contempt for her husband it was unlikely they were sleeping together, and he would have quickly realized the unborn baby was not his own. Infidelity in Colonial New England was a serious offense, and divorce was not a viable option for Bathesheba. An adulteress could be punished by being stripped to the waist and receiving a public whipping of 30 lashes. And for Bathesheba, whose father was a well-known Loyalist, a tar and feathering was not out of the question, either.

When Bathesheba realized she was pregnant she must have panicked and tried to convince Ross that he must kill her husband. The boy was a reluctant co-conspirator, and the murder may never have happened had not fate inter-

---

1 Several articles and a few books have been written about the murder, but my favorite is Murdered by His Wife by Deborah Navas. I have used this book as my primary source for research and quotes.

vened in the form of two British soldierrs, James Buchanan and William Brooks. Both were part of Lt. Gen. John Burgoyne's troops who were defeated at Saratoga and imprisoned by the Americans. Prison camps had lax security at the time, and it was common for British soldiers to escape and try to make their way north to Montreal.

Buchanan and Brooks escaped and were passing through Brookfield where Bathesheba befriended them, much as she had done with Ross. Over a period of several days she somehow convinced all three men to kill her husband, promising she would pay them from her husband's savings.

Author Deborah Navas points out how desperate Bathesheba must have been on the night of the murder. Bathesheba made no effort to fabricate an alibi or even conceal the crime from her servants. The plan was simply to have the soldiers kill her husband, and somehow everything would work out.

On the night of March 1, 1778 the conspirators put their senseless plan into action. While Joshua was at Cooley's Tavern, Brooks hid by the garden gate at the Spooner home while Bathesheba waited in the sitting room with Ross and Buchanan. Brooks must have heard Joshua climb the four granite steps from the road to the yard, then open the gate. That's when Brooks sprang on the unsuspecting Joshua, who was said to cry out, "What is the matter!?" followed by a last terrified scream of, "Murder!" Brooks first beat him with his fists then strangled him. Ross and Buchanan then came out and dumped Joshua into the well headfirst.

The unstable condition of Bathesheba's mind became evident when the men returned to the house. She climbed the stairs to get her husband's money, and when she passed a servant she commented that she hoped Mr. Spooner was in heaven. Minutes later she instructed her two servants to go to the well to fetch water, apparently forgetting where Ross and Buchanan had put the body. When one of the servants came back from attempting to lower the bucket into the well, he said to Bathesheba, "I am afraid your husband is in the well." Bathesheba replied that it wasn't true.

But it was all too true, and when Brooks, Ross, and Buchanan made their escape to Worcester they were arrested as soon as word of Mr. Spooner's murder reached the city. They immediately implicated Bathesheba, and she was also arrested. Bathesheba was still at her house with the sheriff when the body was later dislodged from the well, and she commented, "poor little man."

Trials came about quickly in the 1700's and just five months after the crime, all four murderers were sentenced to death by hanging. Bathesheba, who was pregnant, pleaded to have her execution delayed until after the baby was born. Court officials had her examined by midwives, and their conclusions were mixed as to whether she was pregnant or not. The State of Massachusetts decided to deny her request for a stay, and Bathesheba was marched to the gallows. All reports expressed how calm and unafraid she appeared as she was paraded by hundreds of gawkers who had come to see the hanging.

A post-execution autopsy revealed that Bathesheba was in fact carrying a five-month-old fetus, confirming that the tragedy had claimed another victim.

Visiting the Well and Joshua Spooner's Gravesite

The foundation of the Spooner house and the well where Mr. Spooner's body was dumped can be found on East Main Street in Brookfield. From Route 9, follow Route 148 North about half a mile to where it splits, and bear right on East Main Street. Just after the split, look for four granite steps going up a small hill on the left side of the road. Climb these steps and you will be at the site of the house. The well is just to the right, and is capped by a stone slab flush with the ground. (Beware of poison ivy.) From the looks of the well, Mr. Spooner must have been a small man to have fit inside.

Mr. Spooner's gravestone is located at a cemetery on Route 9, just a short distance from Brookfield common. When you enter the cemetery, stay to the left and follow the stone wall to the limestone tombstone. The inscription reads: *Joshua Spooner, Murdered March 1, 1778 by three soldiers of the Revolution, Ross, Brooks, and Buchanan at the instigation of his wife Bathesheba. They were all executed at Worcester, July 2, 1778.*[2]

---

2 Some historians believe Mr. Spooner's body is not at this site, because his tombstone was placed there perhaps thirty to fifty years after his death. Spooner's gravesite is also rather odd because it lies alongside Bathesheba's sister, Martha Ruggles Tuft, and her husband John Tufts.

THE PRESENT
Exploring Greater Quabbin

"Quick-Guide"
to Greater Quabbin

This Quick Guide will give you an overview of more than 75 points of interest around the Quabbin. It would take dozens of trips to visit all the locations described here, but it is possible on a weekend ramble to make a loop of the Quabbin, making several stops along the way. Before your trip, decide which locations are the most interesting to your tastes, then use this Quick Guide and corresponding maps on your outing. Most of the places in the Quick Guide are discussed more extensively elsewhere in the book.

The four regions, or quadrangles, described below are structured in such a way as to lead your exploration in a clockwise loop around the reservoir, starting at the Visitor Center.

To reach the Quabbin Visitor Center from the Mass Pike, take Palmer Exit 8. After you pay the toll, turn left on Route 32 and proceed north 8.5 miles until you reach Route 9 in Ware. Turn left and follow Route 9 westward. After 5.25 miles there is road on the right with a sign marked, "Quabbin Reservoir/Winsor Dam." If you are interested you can follow this road to the dam, the Enfield Overlook, and Goodnough Dike, but vehicles are not allowed to cross either the dam or the dike. To reach the Visitor Center proceed west on Route 9, crossing the Swift River and take the next right where another sign welcomes you to "Quabbin Reservoir/Winsor Dam" next to a "State Police" sign. Turn right to the Visitor Center, which is a brick building on the right at the end of the dam.

If you are traveling from points north you can pick up the drive at its half-way point by exiting Route 2 onto Route 202 south and then turning left onto Route 122. This brings you to the beginning of the Northeast Region in this Quick Guide.

Once you become familiar with the area, you can spend entire days exploring one or two locations, such as those discussed in detail in the "Hiking" or "Bicycling and Backroading" sections.

Quadrangle Regions

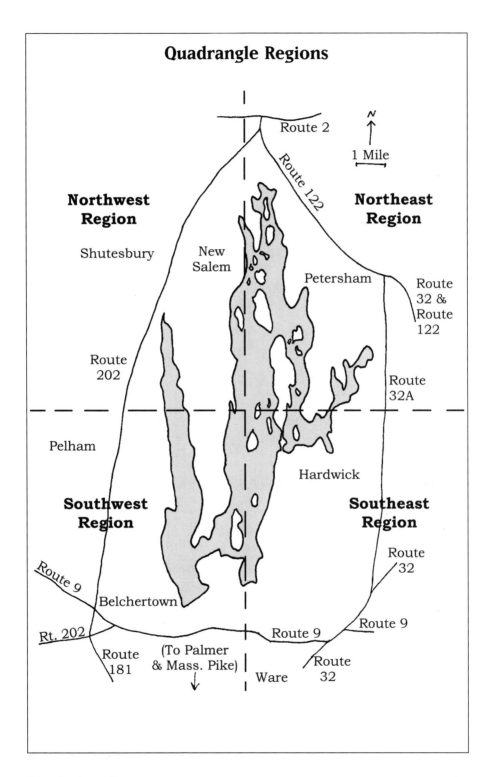

Route 2

N ↑

1 Mile

Northwest Region

Shutesbury

New Salem

Northeast Region

Petersham

Route 122

Route 32 & Route 122

Route 202

Route 32A

Pelham

Hardwick

Southwest Region

Southeast Region

Route 32

Route 9

Belchertown

Rt. 202

Route 9

Route 9

Route 181

(To Palmer & Mass. Pike) ↓

Ware

Route 32

SOUTHWEST REGION
(Ware, Belchertown, Amherst & Pelham)

Winsor Dam and Visitor Center

When the reservoir was created, four towns (Enfield, Dana, Prescott, and Greenwich) had to be evacuated before they were submerged. Learn more about the people who were forced to give up their homes and towns at the Visitor Center (413-323-7221). Quabbin is said to be one of the largest man-made reservoirs in the world created for domestic water use. The Quabbin Reservoir covers 39 square miles, and has a shoreline of 118 miles. Created in the 1930's when the Swift River Valley was flooded, the islands you now see were once the tops of hills!

(In November some of the gates into Quabbin might be closed during hunting season. Call the Visitor Center for details.)

Swift River

Known as the premier flyfishing area of central Massachusetts. Catch and release flyfishing only. The river is always cold because it flows from the bottom of the Quabbin Reservoir.

McLaughlin Fish Hatchery

Children will love it and anglers will drool over the enormous trout! You can purchase food pellets and feed the fish. Thousands of trout of all sizes.

Belchertown

Village green, restaurants, shops and annual Fall Fair in September.

Stone House Museum

A handsome Federal-style home built from field stones in 1827. The museum contains examples of Early American furniture, china and decorative accessories made in the 1700's and early 1800's. Telephone 413-323-6573.

Mill Site and Gate 5

There are the remains of an old mill on Allen Road. The earthen dam supported by stones and a sluiceway are still visible. A pond was formerly located upstream behind the dam, and water was released as needed. Just about every river and stream in Massachusetts had a mill. Gate 5 offers a nice walk (only about one-forth of a mile) down to the reservoir. See the first walk in the chapter entitled, "The Gates of Quabbin and Reservation Walks." (Remember not to leave valuables in the car while you are out walking.)

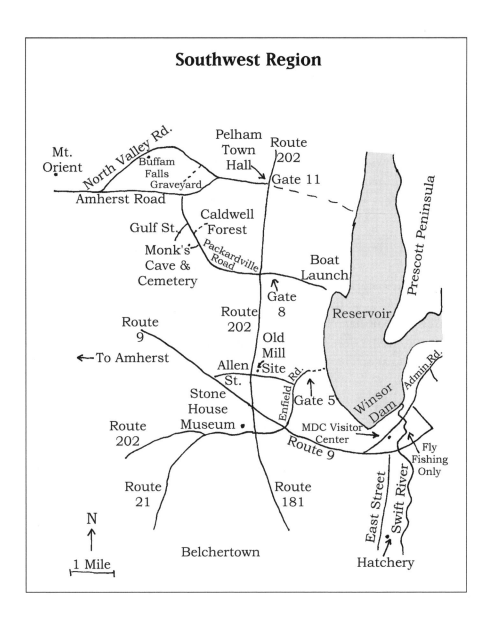

Southwest Region

Mt. Orient

North Valley Rd.

Buffam Falls Graveyard

Pelham Town Hall

Route 202

Gate 11

Amherst Road

Gulf St.

Caldwell Forest

Monk's Cave & Cemetery

Packardville Road

Boat Launch

Gate 8

Route 202

Old Mill Site

Reservoir

Prescott Peninsula

Route 9

←To Amherst

Allen St.

Enfield Rd.

Gate 5

Admin Rd.

Stone House Museum

Route 202

MDC Visitor Center

Winsor Dam

Fly Fishing Only

Route 9

Route 21

Route 181

East Street

Swift River

N
↑
1 Mile

Belchertown

Hatchery

Gate 8

Boat rentals for fishing and a boat launch. Excellent trout fishing. Telephone 413-323-7221.

"Monk's Cave"

Legend says the small cave by the graveyard was once used by monks. If you turn off Route 202 and head northwest on Packardville Road, the "monk's cave" is located in a graveyard about a mile north of the sign that says, "Cadwell Forest." The graveyard is not clearly visible from the street—it's about 200 yards down a dirt road to the west. When you walk toward the graveyard do not enter, but instead go the right and follow a short path through the woods. The cave has only a two-foot opening and is located about 50 feet from the corner of the graveyard. It is circular inside, and is about five feet wide by four feet high. Many have wondered if it is a "monk's cave" or an oddly shaped root cellar.

Pelham

Highlights include an interesting 1839 Congregational Church (now home of the Pelham Historical Society), an old burying ground, and a 1743 white town hall said to be the oldest in continual use in all New England. Pelham was the home of Daniel Shays and the center of his rebellion (1786-87) over unfair taxation. The Pelham Historical Society Museum (usually open Sunday afternoons in the summer) houses a rare "poison oyster" epitaph headstone.

Old Graveyard

Some unusual inscriptions are on the headstones from the 1700's and 1800's. The graveyard is difficult to find: from Pelham turn right off Amherst Road onto Valley Road and proceed 0.4 mile to a narrow dirt road on the left. Walk or drive down the dirt road about 300 feet to the graveyard.

Buffam Falls

Series of cascading waterfalls and trails in a forest of hemlock with understory of mountain laurel. Excellent wildlife habitat. Nearby to the west there is more hiking available at Mount Orient.

Beautiful New Salem Common has impressive twin spires.

NORTHWEST REGION
(Shutesbury & New Salem)

Shutesbury
Quiet hilltop village and green. An old church, town hall, and little red library grace the town center.

Shutesbury State Forest
Woodland trails.

Gate 22
Nice walk through hilly terrain down to the reservoir. Hop Brook winds through woods.

Hamilton Orchards
Pick your own apples and berries. Maple syrup made in sugar shack. Country store with cider, pies, and goodies. Petting zoo, swings, great views. Telephone 978-544-7039.

New Salem Center
Has this author's vote for the most beautiful village green in Massachusetts; feels like you stepped back in time. Twin spires from two churches (one now a town meeting house), old burial ground, granite hitching posts, and The Common Reader Bookstore (978-544-7039) featuring out-of-print-books. (New Salem is one of the least densely populated towns east of the Connecticut River.)

New Salem Overlook/Nature Trail
Great overlook of the Quabbin Reservoir from a secluded location. A short walk to the right from the athletic fields behind the fire station in the town's center.

Gate 26
From here it is possible to make a two-mile-loop walk which brings you past old cellar holes to the edge of the reservoir.

Bear's Den
Five-minute walk to a picturesque waterfall. Signs of an early gristmill can be seen.

Swift River Valley Historical Society,
Open Wednesdays & Sundays 1-4 pm from mid-June through August, and on Sundays only from September through Columbus Day. Great collection of

QUABBIN: A HISTORY AND EXPLORER'S GUIDE

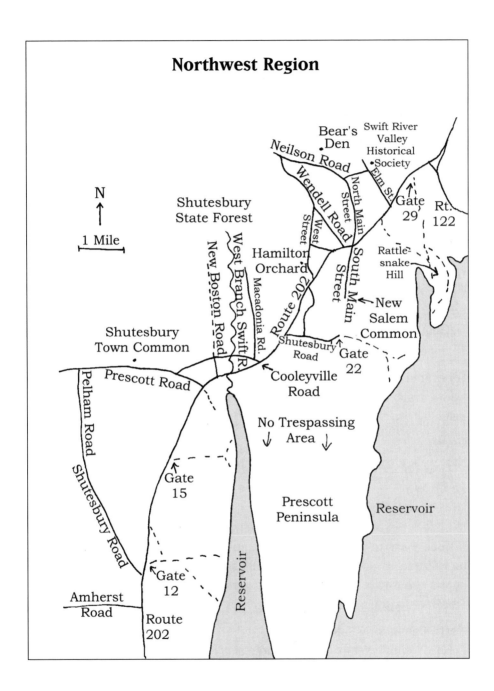

Northwest Region

Bear's Den

Neilson Road

Swift River Valley Historical Society

Shutesbury State Forest

Wendell Road

North Main Street

Elm St.

Gate 29

Rt. 122

N

1 Mile

West Street

West Street

Hamilton Orchard

South Main Street

Rattle-snake Hill

New Branch Swift R.

West Branch Swift R.

New Boston Road

Macadonia Rd.

Route 202

New Salem Common

Shutesbury Town Common

Shutesbury Road

Gate 22

Prescott Road

Cooleyville Road

Pelham Road

No Trespassing Area

Shutesbury Road

Gate 15

Prescott Peninsula

Reservoir

Gate 12

Reservoir

Amherst Road

Route 202

memorabilia from the lost towns, and excellent historical displays. Located on Elm Street about a half-mile from Route 202. Telephone 978-544-6882.

Gates 29 & 30
Here you can walk on old roads to Rattlesnake Hill and the Quabbin, passing by Bullard's Corner.

NORTHEAST REGION
(Petersham, Phillipston & Barre)

Keystone Bridge
Gate 30 features the Keystone Bridge, a stone-arched bridge spanning the Middle Branch of the Swift River, located just beyond the gate entrance. The bridge dates back to the late 1800's. There is a fishermen's trail along the river to the Quabbin.

Gate 31
Boat rentals for fishing and a boat launch. Good trout and smallmouth bass fishing. The Quabbin fishing season is different from the rest of the state, usually beginning after ice-out from mid-April through mid-October. Telephone 413-323-7221.

Federated Women's Club State Forest
Hiking trails & six wilderness campsites. Call the Otter River State Forest headquarters at 978-939-8962 for details.

Gate 35
Nice walk along the edge of the reservoir on relatively flat terrain.

Petersham
Lovely town center with historic homes, some featuring white columns in the Greek Revival style, clustered around a village common and bandstand (a good place to picnic). Because the town never had a large mill complex or railroad station, it has retained its quiet rural character. Petersham boasts thousands of acres of conservation land. Don't miss the Country Store on the town common.

North Common Meadow
Acres of wildflowers slope down to a small pond. A footpath begins by the old Brooks Law Office near Petersham center. Good birding & wildlife.

Northeast Region

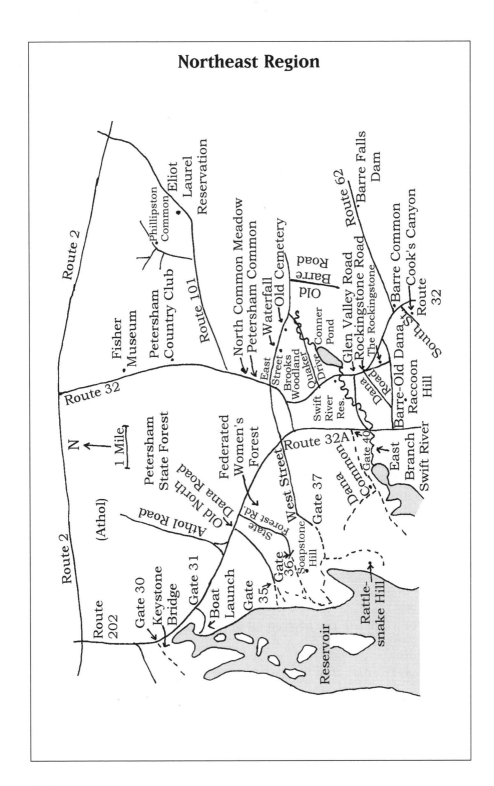

Petersham Country Club
Nine-hole golf course open to the public. Telephone 978-724-3388.

Fisher Museum
Exhibits on forestry and conservation, and models depicting the changing face of New England's forests. Walking trails throughout the property. Telephone 978-724-3302.

Phillipston
Tiny town center with a handsome church. Giant pumpkin contest in autumn on Columbus Day weekend. Telephone 978-249-6828. There are several thousand acres of wildlife management area in Phillipston, just off Route 101

The Red Apple
Pick-your-own apples, pumpkins, and more. Farm animals for the kids. Telephone 978-249-6763.

Eliot Laurel Reservation
Beautiful woodland trails, especially scenic in the late spring when the mountain laurel is blooming. Seldom-used hiking trails.

Brooks Woodlands
Extensive trails through boulder-strewn forest along the East Branch of the Swift River. Excellent wildlife habitat.

Swift River Reservation
Old-growth pines; beaver marsh; trout in the sparkling Swift River; views from ridge top. Excellent wildlife habitat.

Gate 40
A road open only to foot traffic leads through woodland past Dana common and continues to the reservoir. Excellent wildlife habitat. Great birding.

Old Mill Site
Remains of a mill site can be seen on the east side of Route 32A.

Raccoon Hill
State property with a trail that passes a mountain stream.

Hartman Herb Farm
Herb farm where over 250 varieties of herbs are grown. Gift shop. Telephone 978-355-2015.

Rockingstone

Two glacial boulders, one resting on top of the other, are perched on a granite ledge in a seemingly precarious position. However, the boulders are firmly positioned and have probably been so for the past 12,000 years, when the glacial ice sheets retreated and deposited them in this exact spot. On one of the boulders a face is carved which could either date back to the Indian era, or as recently as a few days ago; the folks I asked in the region didn't seem to know.

The massive Rockingstone looks like it can be pushed off its perch.

Barre

One of the larger towns in the area with shops and restaurants. Summer concerts are given from the white Victorian bandstand on the common on Sunday evenings. On Saturday mornings there is a farmer's market on the common. The Barre Historical Society on the common has artifacts, photographs, and textiles. Telephone 978-355-4978. Also in town is the Insight Meditation Center and Buddhist Study Center.

Barre Falls

Dam and conservation area with hiking trails. Good cross-country skiing, picnicking, birding and fishing. Telephone 978-928-4712.

Cook's Canyon

A small sanctuary with trails leading through a meadow and forest to a scenic pond. A great walk along a stream.

Old Cemetery

Read the old headstones and learn a bit of history.

SOUTHEAST REGION
(Hardwick, New Braintree, the Brookfields & Ware)

Gate 43

Boat rentals for fishing and a boat launch. Trout & smallmouth bass in the Quabbin; largemouth bass in Pottapoag Pond. Telephone 413-323-7221. Good hiking in winter. Excellent wildlife habitat. Great birding.

Baffle Dam

Heading north at Gate 43 leads to boat rentals, but if you go east at Gate 43 or start at Gate 44 you can reach the Quabbin baffle dam. The road to Shaft 12 beyond the baffle dam is closed for security.

Gate 45

Great walk down to the reservoir, passing beaver dams. There have also been great blue heron nests off a trail half-way down on the right. At the end of the main access road a sparkling stream tumbles into the Quabbin. Excellent wildlife habitat. Great birding.

Hardwick Center

Scenic village green is the site of an old-fashioned country fair every August. Tents, stalls for livestock, and a wide assortment of games take over the town green for the fair. You'll feel like you're witnessing New

Southeast Region

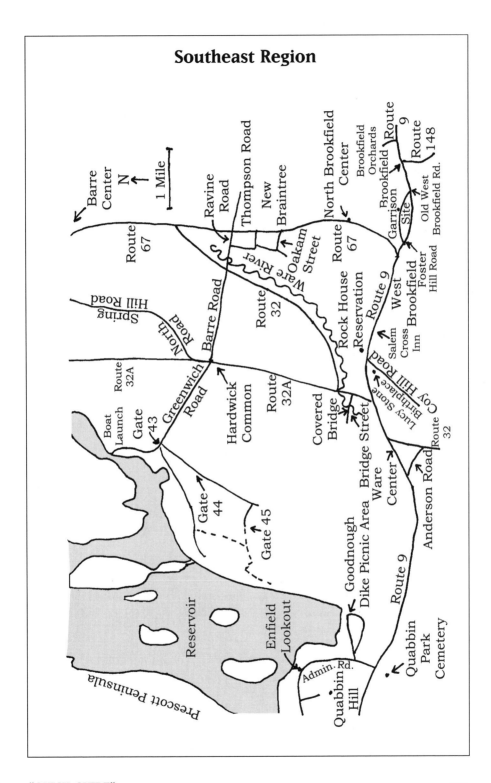

England as it was 70 years ago. Children are sure to love petting the cows, sheep and pigs, or taking a horse-and-wagon ride, and will enjoy the little parade. Telephone 413-477-6197.

Ware River
Trout fishing, canoeing.

New Braintree Center
Quiet town center off the beaten track. Kip's Tree Farm is at the town center—look for the reindeer out by the barn. New Braintree and the Brookfields are loaded with historical markers pertaining to King Philip's War. See the chapter entitled, "Nipmuck Warriors and the Siege of Brookfield."

Brookfield Orchards
Pick your own apples. Gift shop with goodies and crafts. Telephone 508-867-6858.

Brookfield
Charming town green extending south from Route 9. (On future trips, if you want to go straight to the Brookfield area and you are coming from the Boston region there is a shortcut: Take the Mass Pike to the Sturbridge exit (Route 84) then into Sturbridge west on Route 20. Head north on Route 148 to Brookfield.)

Adjacent to Brookfield is North Brookfield, the largest of the four Brookfields. A brick train depot (1875) and many large 19th century homes can be found here.

Foster Hill Road
Scenic country road, with a marker at the site of a dramatic Indian attack during King Philip's War. Benjamin Franklin set a milestone here during the period when postage was charged by the mile.

West Brookfield
Large town common surrounded by handsome homes. Another Benjamin Franklin milestone is found here.

Book Bear
A bookshop loaded with rare and used books. Telephone 508-867-8705.

Salem Cross Inn
Fine dining in a fascinating historic building, with a 1699 beehive brick oven. Hay rides and sleigh rides are available in season on the grounds of this 600-acre inn and farm. Telephone 508-867-8337.

Lucy Stone Birthplace

Lucy Stone was born here in 1818. An ardent campaigner for women's rights, she was ahead of her time, lecturing widely on anti-slavery and women's equality. When she married, she and her husband co-signed a "Marriage Protest," in which Lucy "kept custody of her own person."

Rock House Reservation

Rock overhang which served as a shelter for Native Americans. Trails, pond, nature center, interesting glacial boulders. Excellent wildlife habitat. Kids will love it!

Covered Bridge

One of only a handful remaining in Massachusetts, the Ware Bridge dates back to 1886. It is a 137-foot "Town Truss" bridge spanning the Ware River.

Ware

The largest town on the tour. Plenty of shops and restaurants.

Quabbin Park Cemetery

Before the reservoir was flooded, all the graves in the area were exhumed and reinterred at this cemetery.

Goodnough Dike Picnic Area

Open, sunny areas where you can picnic with a view. The vista from the Goodnough Dike is better than that from the Windsor Dam. Open to pedestrian access across the top of the dike, but closed to motor vehicles.

Enfield Lookout

From here, you can look down to the location where the town of Enfield once stood. A winter visit may offer an opportunity to see a bald eagle from this spot.

Quabbin Hill

Sweeping views of the reservoir and surrounding hills from Quabbin Summit Tower.

Quabbin Rules and Regulations

Quabbin has strict rules and regulations, some of which are perplexing. But on the whole, these rules make Quabbin special and keep it first and foremost a drinking water supply, which in turn keeps it natural. I prefer to see the rules remain as they are. Once one rule is amended for a recreation group, other groups will surely seek additional exceptions; and the next thing you know, the Quabbin will be no different from a state park.

Think of Quabbin as a place to tread softly. There is no snowmobiling, no pleasure boating, no camping, no pets, and all these rules help make it what it is—peaceful. It's one of the few places one can simply enjoy solitude and silence.

These are the Metropolitan District Commission rules for the Quabbin Reservation:

1. Entrance or exit from the Quabbin Reservation shall be made over designated areas only.

2. No person is allowed within the reservation before one hour prior to sunrise or after one hour past sunset unless authorized with a written permit from the Commission. Night access is allowed seasonally with permit through Gates 16, 31, 33, 35, 41, and 43 only.

3. All acts which pollute the water supply are prohibited. No litter or refuse of any sort may be thrown or left in or on any land or water within the reservation.

4. All acts which injure the property of the Commonwealth are prohibited. No person shall injure, deface, destroy, remove or carry off any property, real or personal, under the control of the MDC. Possession or use of metal detectors is prohibited.

5. Fires and cooking are prohibited.

6. No person shall wade or swim in the reservoir or its tributaries. Sporting activities shall be allowed only at such times and in such areas as are designated.

7. Persons 16 years of age or over who possess state fishing licenses will be allowed to fish from shore and from boats at the Quabbin in designated areas. Reasonable fees for the use of boats, for rental of outboard motors for fishing purposes, or use of Commission facilities including parking, may be charged by the Commission.

8. Boats shall not be placed in the water or landed except at designated mooring areas during the season specified for fishing.

9. Violations of rules and regulations will be deemed sufficient cause for revocation of fishing privileges for a period of time not to exceed the current fishing season. The MDC and its employees are not responsible for any damage or loss of life which may be incurred with the public use of the reservation.

10. Drunkenness, breach of the peace, profanity, or other disorderly conduct offensive to the general public is strictly forbidden. Possession of, or drinking of alcohol beverages is forbidden.

11. No one shall drive any motorized vehicle, including snowmobiles, trail bikes, motorcycles, and all-terrain vehicles within the Quabbin Reservation except on those roads authorized for such use.

12. Pedestrian access is permitted through Gates 3A-16 and 22-55. Parking is not permitted in front of the gates or in areas which inhibit access by official vehicles.

13. No persons shall bring any animals, including horses, dogs and cats, into the reservation, unless authorized in writing by the Commission.

14. Bicycles are permitted on paved roads only.

15. Parades, games, fairs, carnivals, bazaars, gifts or solicitations for raising or collecting funds shall not be permitted without written permission from the Commission.

16. Lotteries, raffles, gambling and games of chance are prohibited. No person shall have possession of machinery, instruments, or equipment of any kind for use in the reservation.

17. No person shall engage in any business, sale or display of goods or wares without written permission from the Commission.

18. Public assemblies of more than 25 persons shall not be allowed without a written permit from the Commission.

19. Commercial signs and advertising are prohibited in the reservation.

20. No persons, unless authorized by law or having a valid hunting permit specifically for the Quabbin Reservation, shall have possession of, or discharge any weapon, firearm, firework or other explosive.

21. No one may hunt, shoot, trap, or feed animals or birds in the reservation except with written permission from the Commission.

22. All persons entering the reservation shall be responsible for knowing and obeying these Rules and Regulations. All persons shall obey the lawful directions of regulatory signs, police officers or persons in charge, or of Federal, state or local wardens, rangers or enforcement officers.

Security Announcement

As a result of the tragic events of September 11th, the MDC has increased levels of security at the Quabbin Reservation. Additional water testing, coupled with increased surveillance and patrols by the Massachusetts State Police, MDC Watershed Rangers and the National Guard have resulted in a more secure water supply. Although most of the Quabbin Reservation has been reopened to public access, national or world events may trigger the closure of portions of the reservation. Visitors are encouraged to check the MDC website at www.state.ma.us/mdc/water.htm or the Visitor Center information line (413-323-7221) for updated information. Visitors are encouraged to assist the MDC and the State Police by reporting things which seem out of the ordinary or might indicate an environmental quality problem. This list may include unauthorized persons or vehicles in no-trespassing or restricted access zones, access gates left open or unlocked, or persons carrying suspicious materials or acting strangely. Fish kills, strange materials or odd environmental conditions are also noteworthy and should be reported. Information can be passed along to a number of different sources; personnel will see that it is delivered to the appropriate staff. The State Police Barracks at Quabbin Reservoir is staffed 24 hours a day and can be reached at (413) 323-7561. The MDC Watershed Rangers phone number is (413) 323-0191, although they don't always have personnel to answer the phone. Information can also be given to the Visitor Center staff (413) 323-7221, or the Quabbin Administration Office (413) 323-6921.

Walking the Gates of Quabbin and Reservation

The Quabbin Reservoir is ringed by a series of entrance roads blocked by numbered "gates" which exclude vehicles. Most people refer to each entrance road by its gate number. There are fifty-five gates in total, and Gates 3A-16 and 22-55 are open to hiking. Bicycling is only allowed on access road gates that are paved. (I was never able to locate Gate 23 and contacted the MDC. They confirmed that there is no Gate 23; apparently, it was skipped over or possibly combined with another gate, but no one knew why. Yet another Quabbin mystery!)

In the winter most gates are plowed, making the walking easy. If you want to go off-trail, however, its a good idea to bring snowshoes—there's nothing like viewing the smooth curves of snow blanketing stone walls, streams, and fallen trees. (Cross-country skiing is not allowed inside any gate.)

A view of the reservoir from the end of the path at Gate 16.

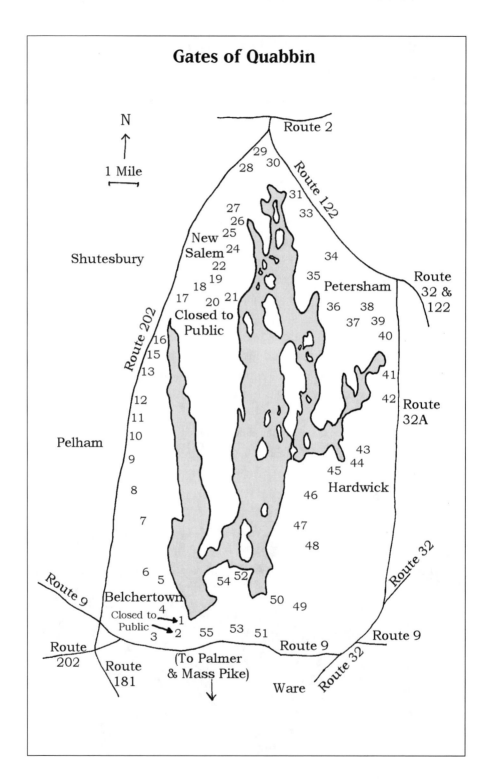

Gates of Quabbin

N
↑

1 Mile

Route 2

29
28 30

Route 122

31
33

27
26
New 25
Salem 24
22
18 19
17 20 21

Closed to
Public

34

35

Petersham

36 38
37 39
40

Route
32 &
122

Shutesbury

Route 202

16
15
13

12
11
10
9

8

7

Pelham

41
42

Route
32A

43
44
45

46

Hardwick

47
48

6 5

Belchertown

Closed to
Public 4
3 1
2 55 53 51

54 52

50 49

Route 9

Route 32

Route 9

Route 9

Route
202

Route
181

(To Palmer
& Mass Pike)

Route 9

Route 32

Ware

Route 32

I've walked the roads and trails associated with most of the gates, but not all, and it's been a fun hobby of mine to set my sights on walking every gate open to the public. Over the last 23 years I estimate I have walked an average of ten miles per month at the Quabbin, which totals about 2,700 miles. Surprisingly, I've never been bored, because each gate has a unique "personality," whether it be the terrain, the views of the reservoir, or the types of wildlife I'm likely to see.

Here I've selected several Quabbin gates that I believe offer some of the most wonderful walking anywhere. I've tried to choose walks that offer a variety of distances, views, terrain and points of interest. Read through them to select a gate that offers trails that meet your desires, and don't be afraid to explore on your own.

Selected Gates and Reservation Walks
(Clockwise Around the Reservoir)
(Symbols indicate which quadrant of Quabbin the gates are located on: SW=Southwest, NW=Northwest, NE=Northeast, SE=Southeast.)
Gate 5 (SW)
Gate 11 & 12 (W-SW)
Gate 15 (NW)
Gate 16 (NW)
Cooleyville Loop (NW)
Gate 22 (NW)
Gate 26 (NW)
 New Salem Academy Nature Trail and Overlook (NW)
Gate 30 (NE)
Gate 35 (NE)
Gate 36 and the Women's Federated Forest (NE)
Gate 40 (NE)
Gate 43 and the Baffle Dam Hike/Bike Ride (E-SE)
Gate 45 (SE)
Gate 47 (SE)
Quabbin Park Trails:
       Quabbin Hill
       Trail From Enfield Lookout
       Quabbin Stewardship Demonstration Trail

Directions to the parking area at the entrance of each gate are given at the end of each review.

Gate 5

This gate is for walkers that want a very short stroll down to the reservoir from a location not far from the Visitor Center. The walk takes about ten minutes from the gate and brings you to a point overlooking the tip of the Prescott Peninsula and the Enfield Lookout. The village of Enfield was directly ahead. Far off in the distance you can see the stone tower at the Quabbin Lookout. When you reach the water you might want to walk north about a hundred feet to the mouth of a small brook. An impressive understory of mountain laurel grows beneath a forest of hemlock, pine, and oak.

Directions: Gate 5 is at the end of Old Enfield Road which runs northeast from Route 9 near its intersection with Route 202 in Belchertown.

Gate 11 & 12

Many people walk a long, three-hour loop from one gate to the other. Park your car at Gate 11, then walk back up Route 202 a half-mile to enter the woods via Gate 12 After walking about three-quarters of a mile down the Gate 12 access road, the road forks and you should go right, following Purgee Brook. Here, hemlocks fill the forest. Follow the path across Purgee Brook all the way to the reservoir, and then return to Route 202 by hiking up the Gate 11 access road (Old Pelham Hollow Road). This long walk is a sure cure for cabin fever come winter, and gives you an idea why many people think of the Quabbin as not just a water supply reservoir, but also a spiritual sanctuary, greatly needed in today's frenetic world.

Directions: Gate 11 is located on Route 202 opposite the Pelham/ Amherst Road in Pelham.

Gate 15

This gate offers the hiker a scenic walk past Atherton Brook, then parallels the Quabbin leading south to where the brook empties into the reservoir.

From this gate, follow the old dirt road south, then bear left (east) and proceed downhill through a forest of hemlocks with an understory of mountain laurel. A quarter of a mile later you will see Atherton Brook on your left at the base of a wooded ravine. Another five minutes of walking takes you past the remains of a large dam made entirely of stone. Atherton Brook passes through an opening in the dam and crosses beneath the road.

Gates 5-7

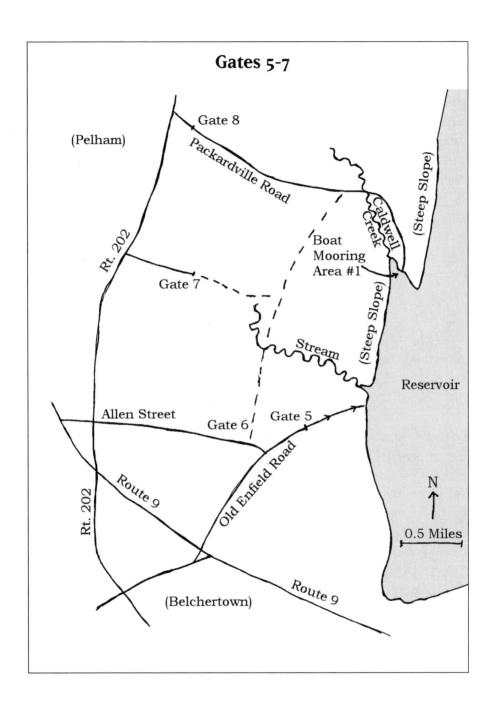

From the remains of the dam, continue walking down the old road, bearing left where a side trail goes right. After a half-mile you will pass three big white pines followed by a stand of small pines in an area that has been logged. Just beyond, is a T-intersection. Our walk goes to the right, southward toward the mouth of Atherton Brook. (If you want a quick peek at the reservoir, bear left and in five minutes you are at the water's edge.) As you head south, the old road passes beneath some large sugar maples, and within 15 minutes you can see the Quabbin through the trees on your left. Some of the hemlocks in the area appear to have stunted tops, indicating porcupines once fed on the tree's branches. Another half-mile of walking brings you to the mouth of Atherton Brook which is a wide marsh area where wading birds and ducks sometimes congregate. The old roadway disappears into the water but offers a nice southern view of the reservoir. This is also a good place to soak up the sun, especially in the winter. I picnicked here once, and it was so quiet that when I chewed on a celery stick it sounded like an army marching by!

Before you retrace your steps, you might want to follow the brook upstream. There are some truly large hemlocks shading the stream, making it well worth the bushwhacking.

Directions: Gate 15 is located about 2 miles north on Route 202 from the Amherst/Pelham Road at Pelham.

Gate 16

Gate 16 provides an easy access point to the waters of the reservoir opposite the Prescott Peninsula. Start your walk at the gate, and after going 100 feet there will be an intersection where you should bear right. It's about a half mile to a fork in the road where you should bear left. The reservoir is only about 600 feet down the road. The water before you is a "finger," or cove, of the reservoir that begins a short distance to the north where the West Branch of the Swift River enters the reservoir.

There are commanding views to the south. On my last trip here in December I had the thrill of watching an otter hunt. Ice had formed inside the north end of the cove and ended where the Gate 16 access road meets the water. The otter brought food (perhaps fish or mussels) from the bottom of the reservoir, then climbed on the ice to eat his or her meal. Even without binoculars it was fascinating to watch, and it's surprises like this that keep me coming back to the Quabbin!

For complete solitude, save this gate for the early spring and fall, because

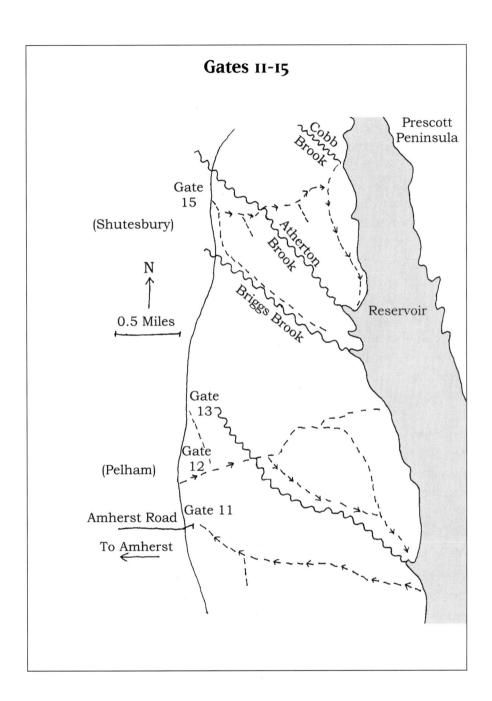

Gates 11-15

Prescott
Peninsula

Cobb
Brook

Gate
15

(Shutesbury)

Atherton
Brook

N

Briggs Brook

Reservoir

0.5 Miles

Gate
13

Gate
12

(Pelham)

Gate 11

Amherst Road

To Amherst

in the summer boaters are allowed to land here for a 10-minute period to utilize the portable toilets.

Directions: Located directly opposite the "Shutesbury" sign/Prescott Road on Route 202.

Cooleyville Road Area

This dirt road has some residential homes on it, but if you follow it down to where it crosses the West Branch of the Swift River it becomes quiet, secluded and scenic, with a couple of gated roads through MDC land suitable for hiking. You can drive to the hiking trails or bike the Cooleyville loop described here.

Drive or bicycle down "Cooleyville Road 184-151" opposite Gate 17 and proceed about 500 feet, then turn left (also Cooleyville Road) until you reach the first bridge, with a beaver pond on the left and a stream on your right. There will be a gated dirt road on your right heading north that is good for hiking. You will see evidence of beaver handiwork in the stream adjacent to the first part of the gated dirt road.

If you continue driving farther down Cooleyville Road you quickly pass over the West Branch of the Swift River, where there is more opportunity for exploration. About a half-mile farther down is New Boston Road on your right, which is gated about 500 feet down, and is an interesting road to walk as it heads north into Shutesbury State Forest. This is very hilly, rugged terrain, especially to the west of New Boston Road along Camel Brook.

If you wish to make a loop and end back on Route 202, continue driving or bicycling on Cooleyville Road. This road goes mostly uphill, passing a red pine plantation on the right, thick stands of mountain laurel, and continueing over Camel Brook. 2.2 miles from the start, you will intersect with Prescott Road where you should turn left (if you go right you enter the hilltop village center of Shutesbury). Follow Prescott Road mainly downhill for about a mile and you will be back on Route 202.

Directions: Drive down "Cooleyville Road 184-151" opposite Gate 17, and proceed about 500 feet, then turn left (also Cooleyville Road) until you reach the first bridge. You can park on the shoulder of the road.

Gate 22

From the entrance of Gate 22, it's about two miles of walking down a dirt road to reach the reservoir. One of the highlights of this walk is the sparkling waters

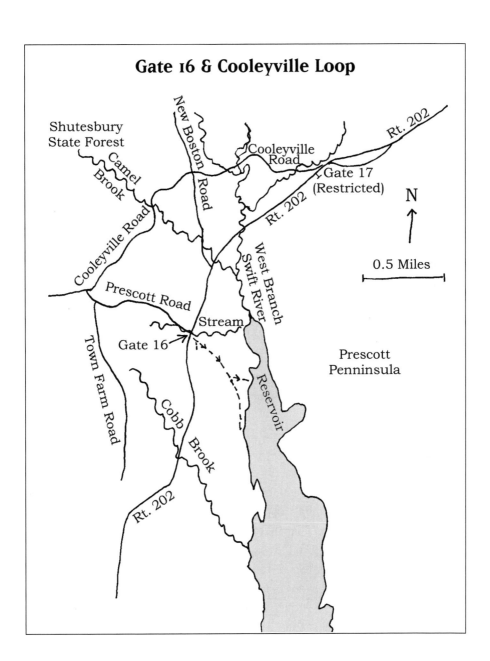

Gate 16 & Cooleyville Loop

Shutesbury
State Forest

Camel
Brook

New Boston Road

Cooleyville
Road

Rt. 202

Gate 17
(Restricted)

N

Cooleyville Road

Rt. 202

0.5 Miles

Prescott Road

West Branch
Swift River

Stream

Gate 16

Prescott
Penninsula

Town Farm Road

Cobb
Brook

Reservoir

Rt. 202

of Hop Brook, which you will cross just an eighth of mile from the beginning of the gate. The village of Puppyville was located just beyond the area where the dirt road crosses Hop Brook. Except for an old foundation or two, the woods of oak, pine, hemlock and maple have now taken over the village. Continue in an easterly direction, staying straight on the main entrance road, and after a mile and a half of walking bear right where the road forks. Another quarter-mile you will again intersect Hop Brook where it tumbles into the Quabbin. This is a fine place to stop and listen to the sound of rushing water and look over the open expanse of the reservoir. The scene to the south is especially breathtaking, with views of islands such as Russ Mountain and "Mount L," both of which were hill-tops before the reservoir was created.

On my last trip in late October, I walked the shoreline and came upon 50 ducks in the reservoir. They took wing when they saw me, their beating wings breaking the silence. At the same time the ducks took off the sun broke through the clouds, casting the reservoir in a silvery light with dark purple-blue hills enclosing the scene. I looked south at the play of light over Russ Mountain, and vowed to make this hike once every winter.

Hikers will also be rewarded by following Hop Brook upstream through the woods as it tumbles through a ravine covered with large hemlocks and pines.

Directions: To reach Gate 22, drive down Shutesbury Road (off Route 202 in New Salem) toward the reservoir for .5 mile to the intersection with Prescott Road, and then bear left continuing on Shutesbury Road for .2 mile to the gate.

Gate 26

Walk past the gate and go straight, passing a dirt road on the right. The road you are on gradually goes downhill. Just before an intersection (about 3/4 mile from the start) there are stone cellar hole foundations on the right. Look for three small cement steps adjacent to the road; these steps were part of Elisha Vineca's property which included a twelve-room home and two barns. A few old sugar maples are scattered about the cellar holes.

At the intersection, go straight about 300 feet to reach the reservoir. Here is a pleasing view of some islands. An even better view awaits you if you walk a short distance south along the edge of the water to a tiny point of land.

To complete this loop, return to the intersection where you bear right to the north. (If you were to go left, the road follows the reservoir south for about a

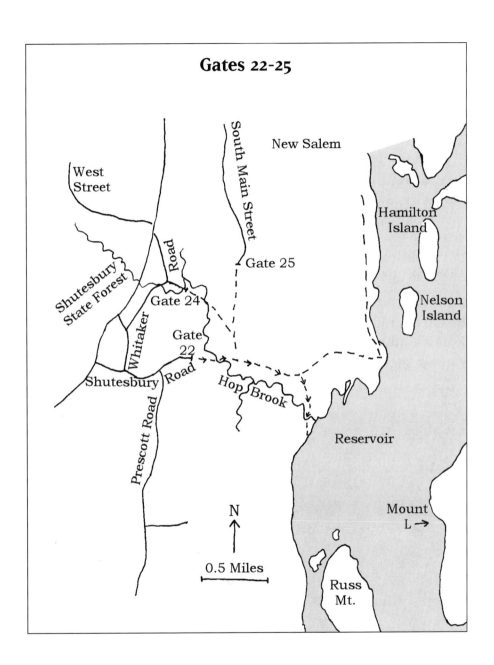

Gates 22-25

West Street

New Salem

South Main Street

Hamilton Island

Shutesbury State Forest

Road

Gate 25

Nelson Island

Gate 24

Whitaker

Gate 22

Shutesbury Road

Hop Brook

Prescott Road

Reservoir

Mount L →

N ↑

Russ Mt.

0.5 Miles

mile). Heading north, follow the road, with the water on your right. The road then curls to the left heading uphill. Another cellar hole is on your right about half a mile farther. At the next intersection turn left and you will arrive at Gate 27, then turn left and you should be able to see your car at Gate 26. This walk is about two miles.

Directions: From Route 202, follow East Main Street (Millington Road) .8 mile to its end, passing Gate 27 on the left, and you will arrive at Gate 26.

New Salem Academy Nature Trail and Overlook

The walk to the overlook is only about an eighth of a mile, so this is a good choice for people who are mobility impaired, or for families with young children. Best of all there are two picnic tables at the edge of the overlook. Views to the east encompass several islands (Nelson and Hamilton islands) in the reservoir. A side trail meanders from the main trail for more exploration.

Directions: Take South Main Street into New Salem Center and drive on the dirt road behind the fire station down to the athletic fields. Keep the athletic fields on your left and follow the dirt road to the parking lot. A wide gravel path brings you to the overlook.

A picnic bench and view of the Quabbin awaits hikers at the New Salem Nature Trail and Overlook

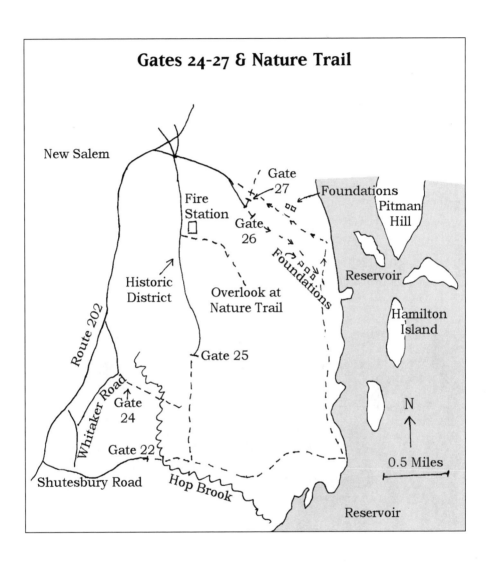

Gates 24-27 & Nature Trail

New Salem

Fire Station

Gate 27

Foundations

Pitman Hill

Gate 26

Historic District

Overlook at Nature Trail

Foundations

Reservoir

Hamilton Island

Route 202

Gate 25

Whitaker Road

Gate 24

Gate 22

N

0.5 Miles

Shutesbury Road

Hop Brook

Reservoir

Gate 30

Gate 30 is at the northern end of the reservoir on Route 122, just south of its intersection with Route 202. Here you will find the Keystone Bridge spanning the Middle Branch of the Swift River, just 200 feet from a parking area at the gate's entrance. Built in 1866, the bridge is a fascinating example of Yankee ingenuity. Large stones, hand-fitted together without the aid of mortar or cement, have stood the test of time since the days when horses and wagons crossed the bridge. The craftsmanship is best viewed by turning off the old road just before it crosses the bridge, and walking southward down a trail that leads to the river. More ambitious hikers may want to follow the river downstream about a half-mile to where its waters meet the Quabbin. It's a pleasant walk where you might see otter and beaver.

If you proceed farther down the Gate 30 access road, you will pass a marsh on the right which you should scan for moose. The access road you are on meets with the entrance road from Gate 29. Continuing on the main road, you will see a few open fields. Old sugar maples line this part of the road. About a half-mile from the start, a dirt road intersects the road you are on. Proceed straight ahead in a southerly direction. After another half-mile, you will pass under transmission lines and will arrive at a sign that says:

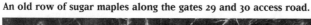

An old row of sugar maples along the gates 29 and 30 access road.

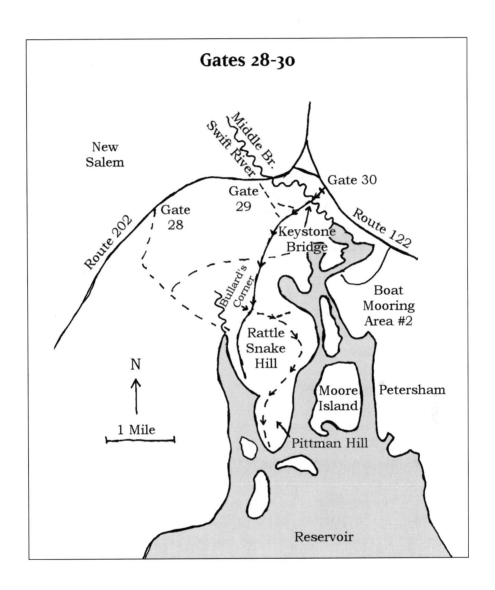

Gates 28-30

New Salem

Middle Br. Swift River

Gate 30

Gate 29

Route 202

Gate 28

Route 122

Keystone Bridge

Bullard's Corner

Boat Mooring Area #2

Rattle Snake Hill

N

Moore Island

Petersham

1 Mile

Pittman Hill

Reservoir

Just a few feet from where you park your car at Gate 30 is the beautiful Keystone Bridge.

Bullard's Corner, site of Herrick's Tavern, a long-time stage coach stop on the Millington-Orange Road. The tavern supplied fresh horses for the stage and food and drink for travelers. The tavern was consumed by fire in 1912.

An orchard has been planted at this spot, and it is a good place to look for bluebirds and other birds that favor open fields. Turn left down a narrow dirt road that heads eastward toward the reservoir. After a quarter of a mile there is a fork; bear right and the trail brings you southward, with Rattlesnake Hill on your right and the reservoir on your left. There are several exposed outcroppings of rocks on the hill which would have been good denning and sunning areas for rattlesnakes when they were plentiful. There are only a handful of rattlesnakes left in Massachusetts (they are protected as an endangered species), but porcupines probably now live in the nooks on Rattlesnake Hill. A few of the hemlock tops are stunted near the south side of the hill, evidence that porcupines have been feeding on them. Rattlesnake Hill is rugged and isolated enough to have bobcats roaming its slopes; and if there area any mountain lion in the reservation, this would probably be one of their haunts.

The trail soon curves away from the reservoir and passes through a notch separating Rattlesnake Hill from Pitman Hill. Thick stands of mountain laurel line the trail. After traveling past Pitman Hill you will reach an inlet of the Quabbin. Proceeding straight ahead, you will reach a south-facing point of land that juts out into the reservoir. This is an ideal place to sit and soak up the sun in the fall or winter, with terrific views of the reservoir. Snell Island is directly ahead, and I often see loons bobbing in the water off its shores. Along the shoreline below Pitman Hill, giant stumps have been coughed up from the reservoir and now lie bleached on the shoreline. When the Swift River Valley was cleared, all the trees were cut down but their stumps remained and were eventually submerged; over time the water has freed them from the reservoir's bottom. Today, many lie upside down along the shore looking like giant spiders, their roots reaching out in all directions.

You can extend your hike by returning to the sign for Bullard's Corner and heading southwest on the paved road. This road passes a stand of red pines, one of the many areas where the Commission planted trees in the late 1930's and 1940's. Red pines were used to protect the reservoir and provide small logs and posts from their timber. However, they also proved to be great consumers of water, so the MDC is currently thinning them out. This road hugs the side of a ridge above a cove of the reservoir and then it abrubtly stops. On my last visit, a flock of mergansers raced along the water and then took flight.

Directions: Gate 30 is located off Route 122 just a few hundred feet south from its intersection with Route 202.

Gate 35

Gate 35 offers a nice loop walk, with a long stretch of the access road paralleling the shore of the reservoir. On the other side of the entrance gate, the road forks into a paved road on your right and a dirt road on your left. This hike follows the dirt road to the reservoir and returns on the paved road. From the gate, follow the dirt road through a forest of white pine and oak. After walking a quarter-mile you will pass beneath transmission lines, and a quarter mile later you will reach the shores of the reservoir. There was once an observation tower nearby where spotters watched planes from Westover Air Force Base practice bombing runs at the Quabbin during World War II.

The road curves to the south along the edge of the reservoir and offers great views of the water. During low water periods, you can walk along the sandy shore and look at the interesting shapes of driftwood and tree roots washed up from the bottom of the reservoir. About a quarter-mile down the road, the view of the reservoir is obstructed by trees. To return to your car, walk back to the area where the roadway first reached the water, and down the hill to your left you will see a path that heads north. This path takes you across an earthen dam that separates a small pond from the reservoir. My friend Bob Clark, who has walked thousands of miles around the Quabbin, believes this dam was constructed in order to form an ice pond in the winter. Bob theorizes that since the railroad passed by this spot, having an ice house at this location would have made it easy to load the ice on the train for transport to market.

Cross the earthen dam and follow the shore a short distance to the where the paved road meets the shoreline on your right. Just follow this road northeast and you will be back at your car in about half a mile.

Directions: Gate 35 can be reached by turning east off Route 122 and onto Old North Dana Road. Follow Old North Dana Road one mile to its end, and park at the gate.

Gate 36 and the Women's Federated Forest

The parking area used to explore this gate is in the Women's Federated Forest, approximately 1.8 miles down the State Forest Road from Route 122, where parking is available at a T-intersection. After parking, walk west, where you will pass a picnic area and a few camping spots in the state forest. (Camping by permit only.) You will soon pass Gate 36 where there is a map and sign. Proceed straight, and about two miles farther you will reach an intersection where you should turn left. After turning left, the reservoir is just a couple hundred yards ahead. From here you can retrace your steps, or go right (north) along the reservoir for about a half-mile until you come to a road on your right. This road will bring you back to the above-mentioned intersection at the two-mile mark.

Directions: Gate 36 can be reached from Route 122 by traveling through the state forest. The entrance road to the state forest is located approximately 3.4 miles south of the junction of Route 202 and 122.

Gate 40

Another favorite gate is Gate 40, where an old road leads to the Dana common. Cellar holes dot the side of the road, one of which is just outside the gate and was the home of "Popcorn" Snow who lived here in the mid-1880's. The eccentric Mr. Snow also fashioned his own metal casket which had a window built in

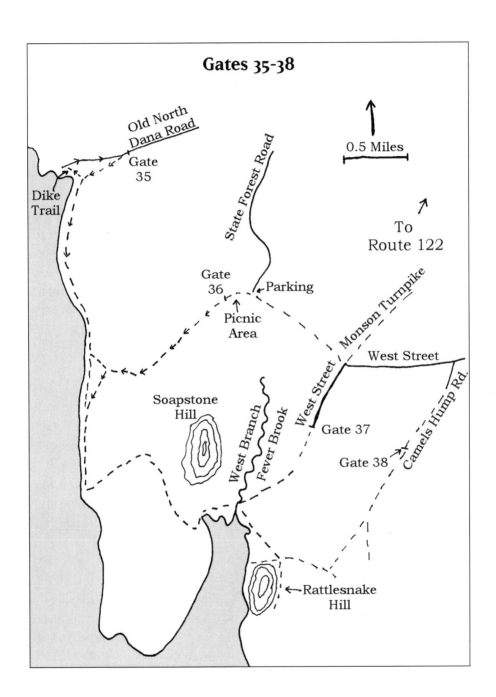

Gates 35-38

Old North Dana Road

Gate 35

Dike Trail

State Forest Road

0.5 Miles

To Route 122

Gate 36

Parking

Picnic Area

Monson Turnpike

West Street

West Street

Soapstone Hill

West Branch Fever Brook

Gate 37

Camels Hump Rd.

Gate 38

Rattlesnake Hill

the lid above the area where his head would lay. This was done so that upon his death he could be checked for seven days after his internment to be certain he was dead! (See the chapter, "A Tour of Dana With Former Resident Earl Cooley," for more details about Popcorn Snow and more information about this gate.)

The walk to the Dana common covers about one-and-three-quarters of a mile down the entrance road at Gate 40. Along the way you will pass a couple open fields where deer are often seen. On your left, barely visible through the trees, is Pottapaug Pond, a large body of water connected to the reservoir. (To see more of Pottapaug Pond, walk down Gate 41; it will take you only 15 minutes to reach the water.) The pond is a good place to see migrating birds ranging from buffleheads to mergansers.

You will know you have reached the Dana common because the road forks, with a triangular patch of grass between the fork. Cellar holes and stone walls encircle the common. Dana common was a handsome place with a church, schoolhouse, post office, livery stable and hotel. When the Quabbin was constructed, these buildings were either removed or razed, timber was cut, and the residents moved elsewhere. Even "Popcorn" Snow and other locals buried in the town's cemetery could not lie in peace; their bodies were reinterred in a new burial ground south of the Windsor Dam.

As you stand at the edge of the common, look to your left and you will see a retaining wall of smooth stones. This was the retaining wall for the Vaughn house, and to the right of that (on the other side of the dirt road) is a large cellar hole where the Johnson house once stood. For more details on Dana Common and the Vaughn retaining wall, see the section on Dana with interviews of former residents. There is a wonderful sugar maple for children to climb by the site of the former Johnson house. Also by this site is another sugar maple; this one is hollow and large enough to stand in. (There is also a seasonal Port-o-Potty a little ways down the road that passes between the Vaughn and Johnson houses.)

At the fork in the road at the Dana common, bear left and walk an additional two-and-a half miles on the main road to reach the shoreline of the reservoir. Along the way you will pass an open marsh that is excellent for birding in the spring. At the reservoir be sure to scan the water and sky with binoculars. In the winter deer are sometimes chased onto the ice by dogs or coyotes, and are killed when they tire. Bald eagles then scavenge on the carrion.

On your next visit to the Dana common, try walking right at the fork at the common. This will also lead you to the reservoir after a two-mile walk. Fellow hiker Bob Clark told me that he once saw a bobcat near the shores of the

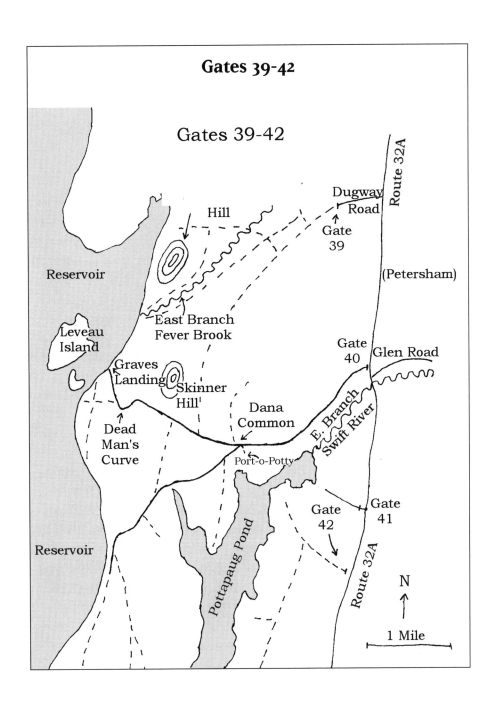

Gates 39-42

Gates 39-42

Route 32A

Dugway Road

Gate 39

Hill

Reservoir

(Petersham)

East Branch Fever Brook

Leveau Island

Gate 40   Glen Road

Graves Landing

Skinner Hill

Dana Common

Dead Man's Curve

Port-o-Potty

E. Branch Swift River

Gate 41

Gate 42

Reservoir

Pottapaug Pond

Route 32A

N

1 Mile

Quabbin in this area. He said he was able to observe the bobcat for several minutes by talking to it in a soft tone and not walking directly toward it. I've found this technique has worked for other kinds of wildlife, and I've gotten some good photographs by simply talking in a calm voice and not making any sudden moves. (A few years ago Bob also saw a mountain lion in this area, as have other people who live in the region.)

Directions: Gate 40 is located off Route 32A on the east side of the reservoir about 41/2 miles south of Route 122.)

Gate 43 and Baffle Dam Hike/Bike Ride

This walk (or bike ride) is about three miles round trip. (As previously noted, biking is allowed on paved roads within the reservoir boundaries.) Park at Gate 43 and proceed to the entrance road straight ahead (to the west) rather than the entrance to the right (north) which leads to the boat launch. Walk straight ahead on the paved road.

You will pass a beaver pond on the right (beaver often abandon their ponds after their favorite food trees are cut down). Just beyond the pond is a glacial esker in the woods on the right. (Eskers are snake-like ridges formed during the glacial period when streams flowing through the ice deposited silt, causing the ridge to slowly build. When I first saw this esker I thought it was an abandoned railroad bed, but at 50 feet tall it was much too large.)

The dirt road that leads to the south baffle dam is about a mile and three quarters from the start of your walk. It is on your right and slopes down a hill toward the water. Baffle dams are closed seasonally to the public due to the use of the area as a winter roost for bald eagles. Only walking (no bikes) is permitted on the baffle dams up to the southern end of Mount Zion. No access is allowed to the islands. (The chapter "Building the Quabbin and How It Works," explains the purpose of the baffle dams.)

The area to the south where the intake building at Shaft 12 is located is permanently closed to the public. Shaft 12 was a setting in Stephen King's horror novel, *Dreamcatcher*. King explained that the Intake Building at Shaft 12 isn't locked, and is a frequent stopping place for lovers in canoes. Readers, however, must remember that *Dreamcatcher* is a work of fiction and the area near Shaft 12 is off-limits to the public (even lovers), and canoeing is not allowed on the Quabbin.

Another possible walk or bike ride heads north from the Gate 43 parking

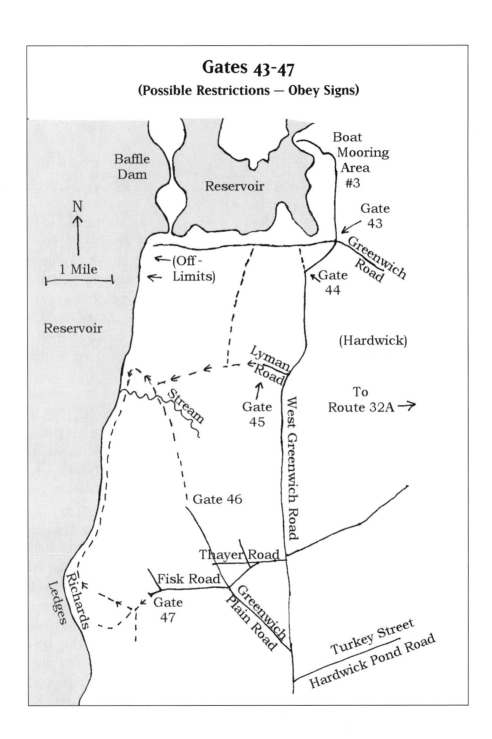

Gates 43-47

(Possible Restrictions — Obey Signs)

Baffle
Dam

Reservoir

Boat
Mooring
Area
#3

Gate
43

Greenwich
Road

N

1 Mile

←(Off -
← Limits)

↖Gate
44

Reservoir

(Hardwick)

Stream

Lyman
Road

↑
Gate
45

To
Route 32A →

West Greenwich Road

Gate 46

Thayer Road

Richards
Ledges

Fisk Road

Gate
47

Greenwich
Plain Road

Turkey Street

Hardwick Pond Road

area to the boat launch at the dam which separates Pottapaug Pond from the Quabbin. I usually see deer when I walk this road in the winter, probably because the many hemlocks provide shelter from the wind. I've also seen several porcupine; they, too, are attracted by the hemlocks because the evergreens are one of their primary food sources.

Directions: Gate 43 is reached from Hardwick center by taking Greenwich Road to its end.

Gate 45

This is one of the less-frequented gates, but it's a good one, leading to a small crescent-shaped beach on the Quabbin where a stream tumbles in.

After parking your car on the shoulder of Lyman Road at Gate 45, go around the gate and start your walk down this old roadway, while admiring the stone walls and old maples. The fieldstone walls that line the road might cause you to reflect on how this land looked prior to the reservoir's creation. Farms and small mills dotted the valley. The land around you was probably pasture before the start of the construction of the reservoir in 1928. Some of the original maples which shaded the road are still standing along the stone wall, while the woods beyond are filled with younger pines and oaks.

After three-eighths of a mile, you will pass an open area on the left—a good spot to look for deer. After walking about fifteen more minutes you will pass a road on your right, about three-quarters of a mile from the start of your walk. You might want to take a side detour down this road (about three-quarters of a mile) to a beaver pond, where great blue herons sometime nest in the dead trees rising from the water.

Back on the main road, proceed straight ahead through a wooded area with many white pines, and pass a beaver pond on the left. Continue to follow the road in a westerly direction. There is a small plantation of red pine on the left before the road curves to the left; here a stream rushes beneath the road through old stone culverts. At the next intersection, bear right and proceed downhill through a dark hemlock grove, while the stream keeps you company. Look for porcupine browsing on the foliage and bark in the hemlocks. After passing a stand of white birch, you arrive at the shores of the Quabbin, roughly two miles from the entrance gate. By following the trail to the left, adjacent to the shore, you soon again intersect the stream where it cascades down the hillside and into the Quabbin at the half-moon beach. Mount Lizzie rises from the water directly across from this beach. Be on the lookout for bald eagles with their incredible seven-foot wingspans.

Directions: From the Hardwick town common follow Greenwich Road 2.6 miles until you reach Gate 43. Bear left at Gate 43 (staying on Greenwich Road) and go 1.7 miles to Lyman Road on the right. Follow Lyman Road 0.7 miles to Gate 45 and park off the road. (Lyman Road can be slippery in periods of snow and ice. If conditions are bad, try Gate 43, Gate 40, or Quabbin Hill near the Windsor Dam.)

Gate 47

This gate is about the hardest to find at the Quabbin, so I only recommend it for "gate fanatics" like myself. This gate receives few visitors, so some readers may want to try it for this reason.

From the gate, the dirt road leads downhill through an oak forest for three-quarters of a mile to a T-intersection. At the intersection turn right to head toward the reservoir. Most of this dirt road is downhill, skirting an area to the west called Richard's Ledge. It's about a mile and a half before the road reaches the water, where it then parallels the edge of the reservoir as it heads north.

Take a moment to walk by the edge of the water and look out upon Mount Lizzie rising steeply from the reservoir. Far to the south you can see the Quabbin Summit Tower.

It is possible to follow the dirt road northward for about three miles to the crescent-shaped beach described in Gate 45.

Directions: From Route 32A in Hardwick take Turkey Street southwest to the juncture with Greenwich Road. Turn right on Greenwich Road, then left on Thayer Road. Take another left on Fisk Road. Where Fisk Road curls right you will see a dirt road that goes straight ahead. After a mile, the dirt road leads to Gate 47. This last mile is rough road.

QUABBIN PARK TRAILS:
Quabbin Hill

This hike is a four-mile loop, and walking is done on both trails and roadways. The trailhead is at the east end of the Quabbin Summit Tower parking lot; turn left and follow the yellow blazes on a gradual northerly descent. After hiking a mile, you will pass a grassy field. Bear left here on a grassy road to an intersec-

At Quabbin Park there are commanding views from the Enfield Lookout.

tion with a dirt road. Head right on this dirt road, and you will soon reach the main road which passes the Enfield Lookout. Follow the main road for about three-fourths of a mile to Hank's Picnic Area. On the right side of the main road directly opposite the picnic area is a gravel road. Follow the gravel road, which passes stone walls and cellar holes. After half a mile turn off the gravel road onto a trail on your right (marked with yellow blazes) which climbs Quabbin Hill and leads you back to the lookout.

Directions: Follow the signs to the Quabbin Summit Tower and park in the large lot.

Trail from Enfield Lookout
This is a circular walk of about 2.5 miles, most of which is through the woods and along the reservoir, but some portions are along the main road to the Goodnough Dike. As you face the Quabbin from the Enfield Lookout, the trailhead will be to your left. Follow the mowed old road downhill, first through a field directly below the Enfield Lookout and then through woods of maple and birch paralleling a stone wall. After it rains, this road can be very muddy. After

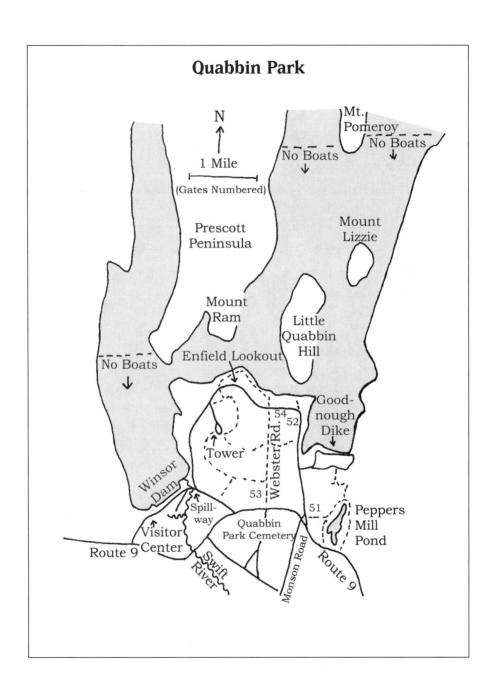

Quabbin Park

N

↑

|— 1 Mile —|

(Gates Numbered)

Prescott
Peninsula

Mt.
Pomeroy

No Boats
↓

No Boats
↓

Mount
Lizzie

Mount
Ram

Little
Quabbin
Hill

Enfield Lookout

No Boats
↓

Good-
nough
Dike
↓

54
52

Webster Rd.

Tower

53

51

Peppers
Mill
Pond

Winsor
Dam

Spill-
way

Visitor
Center

Quabbin
Park Cemetery

Monson Road

Route 9

Route 9

Swift
River

walking about three-quarters of a mile, you will reach the edge of the reservoir at a rocky shoreline; this is a great place to rest and admire the view of the Quabbin. Bald eagles can frequently be seen here, so be on the lookout. At one time an eagle nested on a pine tree on the Prescott Peninsula directly to the west across the water from where you stand.

When you are ready, proceed along the narrow trail set back about 15 feet to your right that follows the shoreline through a shaded area of pines. This trail has roots and boulders on its path, so pick your way along it carefully. There are pleasant views of the reservoir from this trail. The island you will see ahead of you is Little Quabbin Island; its summit is 911 feet, approximately the same height as the Quabbin Summit Tower. After walking about a mile you will enter a grassy area. Turn right up a grassy road to Hank's Picnic Area. From the picnic area, proceed along the road uphill until you come to the main road. Turn right and follow the main road three-fourths of a mile back to the Enfield Overlook.

Directions: Follow the signs toward the Goodnough Dike until you see the Enfield Lookout, and park here.

Quabbin Stewardship Demonstration Trail

This trail has two loops. The upper loop, known as the Vista Trail, is three-fourths of a mile, and the lower loop is an additional half-mile. Both trails have numbered stops and displays that help you understand the changing forest landscape. The forest is actively managed, and the interpretive signs explain why certain forestry measures are in place. You will also learn about types of natural habitats that attract certain wildlife, including threatened or endangered species.

The MDC has an excellent brochure that corresponds with the numbered displays on the trail. The brochures for the Stewardship Demonstration Trail are inside the Visitor Center, so be sure to pick one up before you begin this hike.

Directions: As you face the administration building, the trailhead is to the left.

(Other recommended walks in Quabbin Park include the mile-and-a-half, north-south, woods road called Webster Road, and the trails near Peppers Mill Pond. Both are indicated on the Quabbin Park map in this book.)

Nearby Hikes

The hiking areas outlined in this section are located near the Quabbin but are not within the reservation's boundaries. Some are just a couple of minutes away from the Quabbin, while others can be as distant as a half-hour drive. Ownership of the properties varies and includes The Trustees of Reservations, the Massachusetts Audubon Society, state parks and town conservation lands.

WEST OF QUABBIN
(NEW SALEM, AMHERST, PELHAM, WENDELL)

The Bear's Den (New Salem)

The Bear's Den features a small waterfall nestled in a ravine shaded by towering hemlocks and white pines. Once the site of a mill, the area is now owned by The Trustees of Reservations, and there are hiking trails along the Middle Branch of the Swift River. Legend has it that Metacom, also known as King Philip, and the Nimpuck Sachem Muttawmp gathered their warriors here before attacking the town of Deerfield. Another legend relates how an Indian woman saved a kidnapped Colonial baby by hiding it in one of the little caves by the Bear's Den and notifying the parents. No one can say for certain whether these legends are true or not, but it isn't hard to see why this might have been a meeting place for Native Americans. Besides the river, rock formations and waterfall, there is an interesting overlook above the falls. I had been hiking here for years and never knew about the overlook until a reader of my historical novel, *Until I Have No Country*, wrote to me and said I should check it out. I revisited the Bear's Den, and followed his directions. I crossed the river, headed upstream a few feet past the giant boulder that splits the stream, and then scrambled up the side of the ledge. On top of the cliff was the overlook, which I dubbed the "eagles nest." It's a bowl-shaped depression in the rocks that has an open view looking down upon the waterfall. Three sides of the overlook are surrounded by thick stands of mountain laurel. The tops of the hemlock trees which grow in the ravine below are at about the same height as the "eagles nest." Perhaps this was an Indian meeting place.

The waterfall at the Bears Den turns from a torrent in the spring to a trickle in the summer.

Directions: From Route 2 take Exit 16 to Route 202. Proceed 2 miles to the intersection of Routes 122 and 202 in New Salem, then take Route 202 south another .4 mile. Turn right on Elm Street, travel .7 mile then turn left on Neilson Road. After .5 mile park on the roadside by the Bear's Den sign on the right.

Wendell State Forest (Wendell)

This huge, 7,500 acre property features miles of walking trails, beaver lodges, ponds, wetlands and a brook. One of the better walks is the loop trail around Ruggles Pond. You can also walk a portion of the Metacomet-Monadnock Trail that passes through the property.

Directions: From Route 63 in Millers Falls, turn onto Highland Avenue and follow that eastward for .5 mile to Wendell Road and turn right. Follow Wendell Road for 3.1 miles to Chestnut Hill Road and turn left at the forest entrance sign.

Buffam Falls (Pelham)

Amethyst Brook and Buffam Brook join at this lesser known conservation area called Buffam Falls. The trails along the brooks are relatively flat, making this a good walk for young children. Otter, wild turkey and coyote are some of the animals that have been seen here. Large hemlock trees shade the brooks and a mix of hardwoods and softwoods are found farther away from the streams.

Directions: From the junction of Route 202 and Amherst Road (at the Pelham Town Hall) take Amherst Road west about 2 miles to the United Church of Pelham (where Meeting House Road and Enfield Road intersect with Amherst Road.) From this intersection continue west on Amherst Road exactly 1.2 miles to North Valley Road on the right. Turn right on North Valley Road and go .6 mile to the pull-off on the left under the power lines. If you are coming from Amherst, take Main Street east to where it crosses North East Street and continue 1.7 miles (Main Street turns into Pelham Road). Turn left on North Valley Road and go .6 mile to the pull-off on the left under the power lines.

Mount Orient (Amherst)

This property is located near Buffam Falls, and it's possible to hike both locales in the same day without any hurry. The trail from the parking lot traverses a field, then crosses Amethyst Brook and follows it upstream. Although I've never fished the brook, it looks deep and clear with enough oxygenated water to support trout. Most of the path to the summit of Mount Orient is a gradual climb with only one steep section near the end. At the summit there is a westward view toward the Holyoke Range. I'd estimate the round-trip walk to the summit to be about two hours.

Directions: From Route 202 in Pelham take Amherst Road west and follow for 4.7 miles to the parking lot for Amethyst Brook Conservation Area on the right. If you are coming from East Amherst on South East/North East Road take Pelham Road eastbound and follow .8 mile to parking lot on the right.

Mount Norwottock (Amherst)

The six-mile-long Holyoke Mountain Range is rather unusual in that it is one of the relatively few mountain ranges running east-west in America. While Mount Holyoke receives the majority of visitors because it has an access road to the top, Mount Norwottock is actually the taller of these neighboring mountains. The views are quite different as well: Mount Holyoke offers a spectacular view to the west and north overlooking the Connecticut River, while Mount Norwottock's best vista is to the east, looking out over Rattlesnake Knob and beyond.

Start your outing at the Visitor Center on Route 116, and follow the white markers on the Metacomet-Monadnock Trail that climbs Mount Norwottock. (The entire Metacomet-Monadnock trail is 117 miles long!) As you climb the mountain, notice that hemlock thrive on its north side, where the ground stays more moist and shaded. It takes about an hour to reach the summit, where you can watch for migrating hawks soaring in "kettles" in the spring and fall. At any time of year you can hear the squawk of a raven.

If you follow the white markers of the Metacomet-Monadnock Trail from the summit downhill for two-tenths of a mile, they will lead you to an overhang of rock known as the Horse Caves. You will know you have almost reached the caves, because the trail squeezes through a crevice in an outcrop that leads to the caves below.

These caves were said to shelter tax protestor Daniel Shays and his men and horses during the era of the Revolutionary War. Although the overhanging rock is certainly broad enough to shelter four or five men, I doubt they could squeeze in more than a horse or two. But if you had been on the run, as Shays was for leading a tax rebellion, any shelter would have been welcome.

Children will love the overhanging rock shelter and the nearby nooks and crannies, but the hike to this spot is not easy. If you plan on making a day of it, there is no need to rush, and you can make plenty of rest stops along the way.

Directions: From the Quabbin area at the intersection of Routes 9 and 202, take Route 9 west about 3/4 mile to Bay Road on the left. Follow Bay Road for 6 miles to Route 116 and turn left. Follow Route 116 1.2 miles to the Visitor Center on the left. From the center of South Hadley take Route 116 north for 4.5 miles to the Visitor Center on the right.

NORTH OF QUABBIN

Tully Lake & Long Lake (Athol/Royalston)

Tully Lake and adjacent Long Lake are quite secluded and home to a breeding moose population. In fact, these lakes, in my opinion, offer paddlers the best chance to see moose in Massachusetts. Operated by the U.S. Army Corps of Engineers, over 1,250 acres of wildlands are protected here.

Tully Lake is about 200 acres and studded with pine-clad islands. There is a boat launch, picnic area by the dam, and 24 walk-in tent sites. The lake is inhabited by warm water species of fish such as largemouth bass and pickerel. There are several roads through the woods that are great in the winter for cross-country skiing and snowshoeing. There is also a mile-long trail that leads from Doane Hill Road northward along the east side of Long Pond all the way to Spirit Falls.

Directions: From Route 2, follow Route 32 north to Athol and then continue 3.5 more miles to the Tully Lake office on the left. Long Lake is just to the north of Tully Lake. Telephone 508-249-2547.

Otter River State Park/Birch Hill Dam Recreation Area (Winchendon)

Otter River State Park is a multiple use park that offers snowmobiling and cross-country skiing in the winter, and fishing, hiking, camping and swimming in Lake Dennison.

The Birch Hill Dam Area, managed by the U.S. Army Corps of Engineers, offers hiking and canoeing around the impoundment on the Millers River that was cre-

Jacobs Hill offers a fine view to the west overlooking Long Pond.

ated when the dam was constructed. There are several trails along the Millers River, one of which leads to a scenic overlook known as King Philip's Rock.

Directions: The main entrance to Otter River State Park is on Route 202 in Winchendon. From Route 2 take Exit 20 and follow Baldwinville Road north to Route 202. Follow Route 202 north to the entrance on the left. Telephone 978-939-8962. To reach Birch Hill Dam turn off Route 202 and head northwest on Route 68 to the signs for the dam. Telephone 978-249-4467.

NORTHEAST OF QUABBIN (PETERSHAM, PHILLIPSTON)

If you visit the Quabbin by accessing the area from the east on Route 2, try your return trip via Route 101 which will take you from Petersham through Phillipston and into Templeton, where you can stop at the Ice Cream Barn before getting back on Route 2.

Eliot Laurel Reservation (Phillipston)

Owned by The Trustees of Reservations, a hike at Eliot Laurel will take you through fields and up a forested ridge through acres of mountain laurel. The mountain laurels are near the trailhead, so even if you cannot walk long distances you may want to see these shrubs bloom in the springtime. The property is not especially large and the trail is only a mile long, but because of its secluded location in rural Phillipston this is a good place to see wildlife. My most memorable sighting here was a goshawk, a swift accipeter that can wing its way through even the thickest forest.

Explorers should also visit Phillipston which has a charming village green where the annual October Pumpkin Contest is held. The Congregational Church dates back to 1785 and features an old clock with wooden gears in its belfry. Before the clock was converted to electricity, a 417-pound boulder was used as its pendulum.

Directions: From Route 2 west, take Exit 21. Bear right at intersection, and follow Route 2A west 1.1 mile. Bear left at intersection , and follow Route 101 south 3.9 miles. Entrance is on the right. From intersection of Routes 32 and 101 in Petersham, take Route 101 north 3.7 miles. Entrance is on left.

North Common Meadow (Petersham)

Located just off the town common in Petersham, this beautiful meadow is a great place to hike in any season, especially in late spring when several species of wildflowers are in bloom. The open fields are a good place to see bluebirds, meadowlarks and bobolinks. In addition to walking through the fields, you can visit a scenic pond and marsh.

Directions: From Route 2, take Exit 16 to Route 202 south. Go 2 miles to the intersection of Routes 202 and 122. Take Route 122 south about 8 miles to its intersection with Route 32. Turn left onto Route 32 heading north. Petersham center is about a quarter-mile farther. Just beyond the Petersham town green on Route 32 you will see the Brooks Law Office and North Common Meadow on your right. Pull off the road and park here.

Harvard Forest features a network of dirt roads through fields and woods.

The Harvard Forest and Fisher Museum (Petersham)

Several trails are open to the public at the Harvard Forest including the Black Gum Trail, which has numbered markers to assist those who would like to learn how to identify the various tree species found here. Some of the trails traverse wetlands where ferns, highbush blueberries and red maples grow, while other paths lead through a section of forest that was burned in a fire 45 years ago. Harvard University owns this land where the trees are studied to aid in the better understanding of our forests. The interpretive displays at the Fisher Museum are fascinating, utilizing three-dimensional models to demonstrate the changing nature of the New England landscape.

Directions: From Route 2 take the Route 32/Petersham Exit and go south on Route 32 for 3 miles to the entrance and parking area on t he left. (The Fisher Museum is open weekdays from 9am-5pm year-round; Saturdays and Sundays Noon to 4pm May through October; closed on holidays. Hunting is allowed in Harvard Forest but hunters tend to stay away from the Black Gum Trail.) Telephone 978-724-3302.

The Swift River Reservation (Petersham)

Three separate tracts of land totaling 439 acres comprise the Swift River Reservation, owned by The Trustees of Reservations. The Slab City Tract features a trail following the course of the East Branch of the Swift River. Towering white pines and hemlocks shade the path, and a side trail through an oak and maple forest climbs a nearby hill owned by Harvard University to a scenic overlook. The Nichewaug Tract also has a path along the East Branch of Swift River, as well as some upland trails that follow a ridge in a north-south direction. Located off Nichewaug Road, this tract of land is the largest of the three. The Davis Tract, which is adjacent to Glen Valley Road, has a loop trail through the forest that leads to a hilltop with a partial view of the surrounding countryside.

Directions: All areas are located between Nichewaug Road and Routes 122/32. Slab City Tract: From the intersection of Routes 122 and 32, south of Petersham center, go south on Routes 122/32 and proceed 2 miles to Conner's Pond. Entrance is on the right across from the dam. Nichewaug Tract: From intersection of Routes 122 and 32, south of Petersham center, take South Street .9 mile. Turn right on Nichewaug

Enjoying a snack at an overlook at the Swift River Reservation.

Road and travel 0.6 mile. The entrance is on the left. Davis Tract: From the intersection of Routes 122 and 32, south of Petersham center, go south on Routes 122/32 and proceed 3.3 miles. Turn right on Glen Valley Road and proceed .9 mile to the intersection with Carter Pond Road. Entrance is on the right.

Brooks Woodland Preserve (Petersham)

This large reservation has over five miles of hiking trails through woodland of pine, hemlock and mixed hardwoods. Evidence of old farms can be found in scattered foundations and stone walls. A group of grinding stones used by the Nipmuck Indians can also be seen here. Corn was grown as a staple crop for the Native Americans of New England. It was dried and placed in the hollows of large boulders and pounded with a pestle to form corn meal, which was then made into cakes.

To reach the grinding stones from the nearby roadway, travel down East Street to the spot where the Swift River crosses the road, and park by the pool with the millstone lying by its shore. There is a white house nearby, and a dirt road goes past this house into Brooks Woodland. Walk down the dirt road to the first T-intersection and then turn left about a hundred yards farther to the grinding stones.

There are several entrances to the Brooks Woodlands Preserve, including a trailhead on East Street that leads to the Roaring Brook Tract and another on Quaker Road where a trail follows the East Branch of the Swift River. The river is only about 20 feet wide, but its clear rushing waters sing as it cascades over the boulder-filled streambed, making this a very pleasant walk. Just a short distance up this trail, Moccasin Brook enters the East Branch of the Swift River, and the waters mingle as the combined flow heads toward the Quabbin. The last time I was here I saw three wild turkeys coming down the path toward me before they ran into the woods. A springtime walk is always a treat, because the yellow flowers of the marsh marigold add a touch of brightness to the shady forest floor.

Directions: The Roaring Brook Tract can be accessed from North Common Meadow or by going down East Street .8 miles from Petersham center. To reach the Swift River Tract, follow Route 32 south from Petersham center to the intersection of Routes 32 and 122. Go south on Routes 32/122 for 1.5 miles then turn left on Quaker Drive. There are entrances on both sides of the bridge over the East Branch of the Swift.

Visitors are dwarfed by the rock cliffs at the Rock House Reservation.

EAST & SOUTHEAST OF QUABBIN
(BARRE, NEW BRAINTREE, WEST BROOKFIELD)

The Rock House Reservation (West Brookfield)

Children and adults will love a visit to the unique rock shelter known as the Rock House. A ledge of rock, perhaps 60 feet high, forms a cave-like shelter beneath its overhang, with several nooks and crannies along the splits in the rock. I took my son here years ago and we played hide-and-seek. It's one of the few places he remembers vividly from that time. Native American artifacts have been found beneath the rocks. No doubt this was a perfect place for a hunting party to spend the night if they were unable to make it back to the village. Trails take visitors to an overlook, where a small cabin houses a nature exhibit. You can continue walking for about two miles in a northerly direction, and then return to the Rock House by circling a small pond.

Directions: Follow Route 9 east from Ware center and at the fork for Route 32 continue on Route 9 east for 1.2 miles to the entrance and parking area on the left.

The New Braintree White Oak (New Braintree)

This is one of the more difficult hikes to find because you must park on the shoulder of Barr Road and then walk down an old dirt road called Bridge Road, which runs directly between a red house and a barn, making it look like it's private. Stay on this dirt road for about 300 yards and be on the lookout for a side trail on the right, where a sign says, "No Trespassing After Dark." Take this side trail uphill. Woods will be on your left and a field on your right. After walking about 200 yards, you will see the giant white oak. While its height may not be all that impressive, its girth is. Multiple branches extend in all directions from low levels, shading a huge area underneath the tree. This tree is thought to be the largest white oak in New England. The narrow trail to the tree is privately owned but walkers are allowed to visit the tree.

After visiting the white oak you may want to head over to the Hardwick town common where you can reward yourself with lunch or a snack at the country store. The common is beautiful in its simplicity, and every August the town holds an old-fashioned agricultural fair on the common that features livestock, rides and games.

Directions: From New Braintree center go south on West Brookfield Road, and turn right on Gilbertville Road just past the State Police

New Braintree's white oak is worth the visit.

complex. Continue .8 mile on Gilbertville Road and then turn right on
Barr Road. Proceed .3 mile to the intersection of Pierce Road. Park
here, on the shoulder of Burr Road, and walk to the tree by following
the dirt road between the barn and the red house. You can also reach
the tree by following Gillbertville Road .3 mile to an old road on your
left called Bridge Road that is closed to traffic. Walk up this road,
cross a stream, and then look for a side trail on your left.

Cook's Canyon (Barre)

Cook's Canyon features a ravine where water from Galloway Brook tumbles over a granite outcrop and drops over a series of ledges approximately 100 feet to the bottom of the canyon. The trails used to reach the overlook above the canyon are relatively flat, and the return trail along Galloway Brook is a real beauty, with the rushing water on one side and a forest of hardwoods and softwoods on the other. It is possible to make this hike a loop walk of about one hour.

Directions: From Barre center follow South Street to the south for 1/4 mile. The sanctuary and parking lot are on the left.

Barre Falls Dam (Barre/Hubbardston)

The U.S. Army Corps of Engineers administers this large property where picnicking, hiking, cross-country skiing, canoeing and hunting are allowed. There is also good fishing in the Ware River. At the southern end of the property, there once stood an old prison camp. A trail called Prison Camp Road connects Rutland State Park with the Barre Falls Dam Recreation Area.

The dam was built to prevent flooding such as occurred in the devastating floods of 1936 and 1938. Behind the dam is a dry-bed reservoir, meaning that during normal weather the Ware River is allowed to pass through the dam and water is not impounded. In certain rainy periods, or during heavy spring run-off, the dam holds back some of the excess river water and you may see a lake stretching upstream of the dam. Water from the Barre Falls dam can also be diverted to the Lonegan Intake (about four miles south of the dam) and into the Quabbin Aqueduct to supplement the water in the Quabbin Reservoir if necessary.

Directions: From Barre center follow Route 62 eastward until you see the signs for the Barre Falls Dam on the Hubbardston/Barre Town Line.

The Waterfalls of Royalston

Waterfalls seem to be loved by everyone. They speak to our senses with their soothing sound, the sight of white water cascading over dark rock, and the scent of moisture in the air. They also speak to our hearts, making us glad to view a river running free.

Waterfalls are ever-changing: surging with power in the spring, subdued in summer, framed by a dazzling array of colors in autumn, and sculpted by ice in winter. The water itself can be both mesmerizing and therapeutic... just take a few moments to stare at swirling currents and sun-dappled ripples. Linger at the falls, but explore them as well—sometimes by hiking up their ledges and ravines you are rewarded with a unique view from their crest.

When one thinks of waterfalls in New England, the White Mountains of New Hampshire and the Green Mountains of Vermont come to mind. Massachusetts, however, has a number of beautiful falls, albeit smaller and on a more intimate scale. The best ones, to my way of thinking, are natural falls in a forest setting, the farther from the beaten path the better. Three of my favorites are in Royalston, just north of the Quabbin Reservoir and Route 2.

Doane's Falls are part of Lawrence Brook, which tumbles through property owned by the Trustees of Reservations and is open for all to enjoy. Large pine and hemlocks shade the falls as it surges first under a handsome stone arch bridge and then cascades over a series of granite ledges. The first mill on the falls dates back to 1753, and an old millstone and stone blocks can still be seen. A streamside trail follows along the brook and heads toward Tully Lake, passing through thick stands of mountain laurel.

Directions to Doane's Falls: From the intersection of Routes 2A and 32 in Athol, take Route 32 north 4.5 miles, and just beyond the dam at Tully Lake take a right on Doane Hill Road. Go to the end of the road and turn right. Parking is immediately on the right.

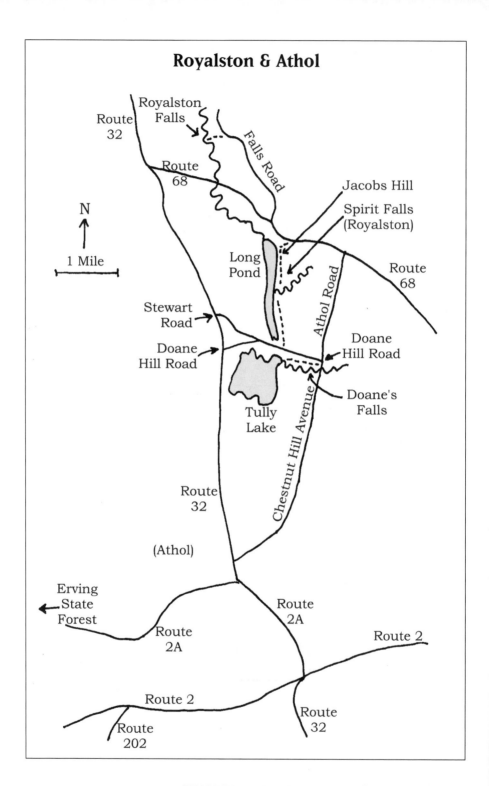

Royalston & Athol

Royalston Falls

Route 32

Route 68

Falls Road

N

1 Mile

Jacobs Hill

Spirit Falls (Royalston)

Long Pond

Athol Road

Route 68

Stewart Road

Doane Hill Road

Doane Hill Road

Doane's Falls

Chestnut Hill Avenue

Tully Lake

Route 32

(Athol)

Erving State Forest

Route 2A

Route 2A

Route 2

Route 2

Route 202

Route 32

Jacob's Hill is another little-known Trustees property located nearby that features a small waterfall and a spectacular view. A fifteen-minute walk will bring you to the crest of a ridge known as Jacob's Hill, where you will be rewarded with a panoramic view overlooking Long Lake and western hills that seem to stretch to the horizon. About a half-mile farther south from the Jacob's Hill overlook is Spirit Falls, a narrow falls but beautiful nevertheless. Here the water tumbles over a series of cascades, passing by moss-covered boulders and towering hemlocks. You can follow the falls downhill by bushwhacking and it's worth the effort to view the falls cascading over ledges and the mist nourishing the ferns.

Directions to Jacob's Hill: From the center of Royalston take Route 68 north 0.5 mile and the Jacob's Hill parking area will be on your left.

The most spectacular falls in Royalston are honored with the town's name, **Royalston Falls**. The falls plunge about 70 feet into a misty little canyon where four-foot-tall cinnamon ferns grow in the shade. This property is also owned by the Trustees, who have thoughtfully put a safety railing at the cliff that overlooks the falls. Visitors who come here during the spring snowmelt will see an impressive display of water pouring over the falls and pounding into the ravine below. This is wild country, home to just about every type of wildlife found in New England including fisher, bobcat, coyote, and porcupine.

Directions To Royalston Falls: From the center of Royalston take Route 68 north 1.4 miles and turn right on Falls Road, traveling 3.2 miles to the trailhead on the left. Note that the last .8 mile of Falls Road is not maintained by the town, so you may have to walk this section; but it's a beautiful stroll past stone walls, old maples and birches.

One of the easiest ways to get to the center of Royalston is to exit Route 2 onto Route 202 north. Follow for 2.4 miles and turn left onto Route 68 north and travel 8.6 miles to the town's center. This austere village green is a real beauty. Because no major roads bisect it, a traveler feels as if he or she has traveled back in time. A church with an incredibly high steeple dominates a long green which is surrounded by handsome white homes.

Water thunders beneath the hemlocks at Doane's Falls.

Photography Tips for Shooting Waterfalls

Sunlight is the key for the best pictures—take a photo in the shade and chances are it will reproduce dull and gray, capturing little of the beauty you experienced on your visit. But finding the right time of day for a well-lighted picture can be tricky. Even on a cloudless day, waterfalls are often shaded because they are usually situated in low ravines, where trees block out the sun. As a general rule, the noontime sun will often light a portion of the waterfall; but if the falls face east, then the morning sun will strike them, just as falls facing west catch the light of late afternoon. Direct sunlight can cause glare, so a polarizer may be necessary. My best shots have come on days when there is some overcast. (For most outdoor pictures, early morning and late afternoon light provides a softer, more interesting, light than the mid-day sun.)

If you have a tripod, try shooting the falls at slow shutter speeds that can capture the motion of the water. Try taking a shot from above the falls, or a close-up of ferns and moss by the water. But in my opinion, the best scenes are the ones we carry away in our memory, and photographs are only a means to stimulate the recollection of the visit.

Bald Eagles

The re-establishment of nesting bald eagles in Massachusetts is one of the Quabbin's great success stories. If you are lucky, you might be treated to the sight of an eagle perched in a pine or gliding over the reservoir. With its distinctive white head and tail, and a massive wingspan reaching seven feet, an adult bald eagle is truly an impressive and majestic bird.

The bald eagle has suffered greatly at the hands of man, first with the pollution of rivers and loss of habitat and then with the advent of the widespread use of pesticides which worked their way into the food chain. The pesticide DDT in particular seriously affected the reproduction of bald eagles by causing the shells of their eggs to thin due to calcium deficiency resulting in embryo mortality. Populations suffered their worst declines in the 1950's through the early1970's. Finally in 1972 DDT was banned, giving eagles and other affected species a fighting chance at recovery. (The banning of DDT was due in a large part to the efforts and research of writer Rachel Carson, author of Silent Spring. Carson was also a federal biologist with the U.S. Fish and Wildlife Service.)

Quabbin Reservoir was the site of the first successful nesting program in Massachusetts since the nesting eagles extirpation. Prior to the Quabbin eagle program, Massachusetts had not recorded a confirmed breeding pair in 80 years, and the only eagles seen were winter migrants or the occasional wanderers.) The Massachusetts Bald Eagle Restoration Project began in1982 when bald eagle chicks were hacked from artificial nesting towers and raised in a feeding program. Babies were fed by an unseen human and constantly monitored. The goal was to produce healthy bald eagles that would then be released and have Quabbin imprinted as their natal area, because eagles have an instinctive tendency to return to the same region upon reaching maturity (usually in four to five years). Between 1982 and 1988 a total of 41 chicks were hacked, and success came in 1989 when two pairs returned to nest and produced three chicks between them.

The Quabbin eagle program was a collaborative effort coordinated by the Massachusetts Division of Fisheries and Wildlife with assistance from the MDC, the U.S. Fish and Wildlife Service, and the Massachusetts Audubon Society. The initial project leader was Jack Swedberg, a photographer and naturalist, who had spent many years hiking the Quabbin and photographing wintering eagles during a period when they were uncommon. After Mr. Swedberg's departure in 1988, the Eagle Restoration Project was directed by biologist Bill Davis who works for the Massachusetts Division of Fisheries and Wildlife. Davis recalls that one of the hardest parts of the project was satisfying the fledgling eagles' appetites. Eagle attendants, often working alone, used three 125-foot gill nets, picking 15 to 20 pounds of fish out of them daily.

Today the eagle project no longer raises chicks, but new chicks produced by wild nesting eagles are still inspected by wildlife biologists.[1] The chicks' diet and overall health are determined, and then aluminum bands are placed around their legs so they can be tracked. In some years up to three chicks were successfully hatched and raised by a pair of eagles, while in other years, such as 1997 and 2001, with unusually cold springs and late-season snowstorms, not a single chick survived.

Eagles mate for life and participate in an incredible courtship ritual where they lock talons in flight and then tumble downward through the air. They build their nests high up in a pine or hardwood tree near the water with large sticks, and line it with dry vegetation and sprigs of pine. Often, the eagles will return to the nest year after year, adding more material so that some nests become quite large. Between one to three eggs are laid each year, and both parents share in the incubation (about 35 days) and feeding (up to 2 pounds of fish per chick per day). About eleven weeks after hatching, young eagles take their first flight.

Eagle Viewing Tips

Perhaps the best time to see eagles at the Quabbin is during the winter months, particularly in February. The more reliable viewing areas include the Enfield Lookout and Grave's Landing (see "The Gates of Quabbin" chapter, Gate 40). Often, the greatest number of eagles congregating at the Quabbin occurs at this time when the intense cold drives them from northern New England. The wintering bald eagles often feed on fish, waterfowl and gulls found in the Quabbin's open waters, or the carrion of deer that have been chased out onto the ice by coyotes or dogs. There are often serious "eagle watchers" braving the cold, and many are more than happy to let you have a look through their powerful spotting scopes. Several times, with the aid of either a spotting scope or pair of

1 By the end of the 2001 nesting season, 126 eagle chicks had been produced in wild Massachusetts nests.

binoculars, I've seen eagles glide over the Enfield Lookout or the Goodnough Dike. At other times I've seen them perched in trees along the shoreline of the Prescott Peninsula, or soaring over Mount Ram. (One time I saw an eagle perched at the top of a tree while a porcupine fed in the same tree twenty feet below.) In the warm weather months eagles are sometimes seen by boaters on the Quabbin or by hikers near the shoreline.

An adult bald eagle is unmistakable with its dark brown body, bare lower legs, large hooked yellow beak and white head and tail. An immature bald eagle, however, does not have the distinctive white head and tail, making it look similar to the much rarer golden eagle. The two birds can be distinguished by the fact that the golden eagle has a smaller head and a hawk-like beak, with broader and rounder wings than the bald eagle. The golden eagle also soars with slightly uptilted wings, while the bald eagle holds its wings on a flat plane.

Sometimes, eagles are mistaken for ospreys, but an osprey has a wingspan under six feet and is far more slender with more white coloring on its breast plumage and underwing than a bald eagle. The osprey also has a noticeable crook in its wing. Ospreys are also migratory and not a nesting species at the Quabbin. Many times when we see a bald eagle winging by with a fish in its talons, the fish was originally caught by an osprey, and the eagle harassed the osprey until it dropped the fish. In cases like this the eagle often catches the fish in midair!

When a bald eagle catches its own fish, rather than by raiding an osprey or by scavenging, it does so by gliding over the water then dropping low enough to skim the surface and snatch a fish with its talons. When ice covers the reservoir, eagles will continue to fish as long as open water is available. The Quabbin freezes quite late in winter, usually toward the end of January. When there is no open water, the eagles at the Quabbin feed primarily on waterfowl and deer carcasses. In warm weather they feed on a combination of fish, carrion and an occasional duck or small mammal.

Other Wildlife and
Wildlife Viewing Tips at Quabbin

Although the Quabbin is best known for its bald eagles, the reservoir provides an excellent habitat for a number of birds and animals that require large tracts of forest and relative seclusion. As noted previously, the Quabbin Reservation is the largest contiguous tract of open space in southern New England. The following sampling focuses primarily on a small array of wildlife not regularly seen in suburban settings.

BIRDS
Owls, Hawks and Woodpeckers
Migrating hawks can be seen in the fall from the Enfield Lookout, Quabbin Hill and the observation tower. The best days for viewing occur during autumn when the wind is coming out of the north or west, which helps to push the gliding birds toward their southern destinations. Balmy days, with the wind coming from the south, or rainy days usually mean that the hawks are resting and waiting to fly when the conditions are again right. Early to mid-September is the best time for hawk watching at the Quabbin. Although broadwinged hawks appear in the largest numbers, osprey, sharp-shinned hawks, Cooper's hawks, American kestrels, and turkey vultures are sometimes also seen. In October look for the migration of red-tailed hawks and red-shouldered hawks. (Many red-tailed hawks winter at the Quabbin and can easily be seen perching on trees over-looking fields.) And don't forget the nighthawks which are the first to migrate, flying south in the early evening in late August. Nighthawks are not raptors, but members of the bird family called goatsuckers which are nocturnal insect eaters.

People are often confused when they see a red-tailed hawk perched in a tree, expecting to see the reddish tail as they look at the front of the hawk. Actually, the tail is a light tannish-white color on the underside with the red on the upperside or back of the tail feathers.

Owls are extremely difficult to spot, particularly in the daytime when the Quabbin is open for hiking. You might, however, see a barred owl perched

A baby great horned owl has fallen out of it's nest near Gate 40.

quietly on a limb about twenty feet up, or see evidence of a great horned owl such as the distinctive white droppings or a pellet at the base of a large hemlock or pine. Owls regurgitate pellets which are the indigestible parts of their prey such as bones and fur. If you are in the woods and you hear crows making a racket, be sure to investigate; oftentimes they are harassing a predator such as a fox, hawk or great horned owl. Great horned owls typically make four to seven low hoots while the barred owl has eight hoots that sound like, "Who cooks for you, who cooks for you all!" Eastern screech owls are also found at the Quabbin. They are considerably smaller than the great horned and barred owls, with a total length of only about eight inches. Their plumage is either bright rusty or gray, and their call is a quivering whistle.

Jack Lash, an ecologist with the Department of Environmental Management, reports that saw whet owls are also common within the Quabbin woodlands. "Their monotonous rhythmic whistling," says Jack, "is best heard at dawn and dusk. The saw shet owl lacks ear tufts and is seven to eight inches in height."

Northern goshawks will prey on other birds, including grouse. You might catch a flash of gray as they pursue their quarry; or during nesting season you might see one perched in a tree, as it signals with a screech that you are approaching too close to its nest. If you fail to heed their warnings, these large hawks will swoop down and dive-bomb you! While goshawks prefer the woods, American kestrels and red-shouldered hawks are usually seen in fields or at the margins between an open area and woods.

Pileated woodpeckers require large tracts of forest, which makes the Quabbin an excellent habitat for them. These large woodpeckers with the distinctive red crest on their head are insect eaters, and their cuttings on the trees tend to be rectangular and oblong in shape. They often chip away at dead trees while searching for carpenter ants. You might be able to hear the drumming noise they make with their beaks, or see one working its way up a tree by taking short hops similar to a squirrel.

Birds That Inhabit Fields and Edges

Woodcocks prefer open fields which are not common at the Quabbin except along certain gates such as Gate 40. In the spring you might be able to observe their courtship flight, or hear their evening or morning call of "Peent!"

In some fields you will see nesting boxes with small openings meant for bluebirds, although tree swallows, chickadees and house wrens also use these boxes. In the late spring and early summer, wait quietly with binoculars and watch the box; you should be rewarded with the sight of a bluebird bringing food to its young in the nesting box. (Several gates have nesting boxes in nearby fields.) Bluebirds are insect eaters and they often perch on top of their nesting box, scanning the fields for food.

Other birds you are likely to see in the fields at the Quabbin are white-throated sparrows and winter wrens.

Wading Birds and Waterfowl

Some of the diving ducks seen at the Quabbin include mergansers, loons, common goldeneyes, and ring-necks. Ducks that feed just below the water's surface but do not dive are called dabbling ducks, and include mallards, pintails, green-winged teal and black ducks. The area around Grave's Landing is a relatively shallow section of the reservoir, and I have had good luck spotting a wide assortment of ducks in this area. Other good spots are the areas where the different branches of the Swift River empty into either the Quabbin or Pottapaug Pond: Near Gate 40 the East Branch flows into Pottapaug, the Middle Branch flows into the reservoir near Gate 30, and the West Branch flows into the Quabbin near Gate 16. During low-water periods, greater yellowlegs, spotted sandpipers and a variety of migrating shorebirds can be seen in the mud flats in the North Dana area.

Wood ducks prefer marsh areas and beaver impoundments rather than the reservoir, and the nesting boxes you might see erected in shallow water are meant to supplement the wood duck's normal nesting cavities in hollow trees. Kingfishers can be found anywhere there is water as they are fish eaters. If disturbed, they make a distinctive loud rattling cry when they take flight, usually flying low over the water or following a river's course.

The Quabbin is the approximate southernmost limit of breeding common loons, and it is an important nesting location for them because the size of the reservoir can support multiple pairs. Even before the reservoir was completely filled, a pair of loons was spotted on the water in New Salem in 1943. The first

A mother loon with two babies on its back.

confirmed nesting pair was found in 1975. Oddly, as of this writing only one pair of loons nest in the area of the reservoir closed to fishing and boating, while several other nesting pairs are found in the unrestricted area. Loons migrate north from mid-March to early June and then head south or move to coastal bays from late August to December. Most loons migrate along the coastline, and in winter it is quite rare to see them at the Quabbin, because they need open water and prefer the ocean.

During the warm weather months at the Quabbin, listen for the loon's unique call to pinpoint it's location. Loons dive beneath the water surface searching for minnows, and they can stay submerged for two minutes. One of the biggest threats to loons is the rise in mercury levels in New England's water.

Turkey and Grouse

Wild turkeys prefer forest and overgrown fields, and if you scan a field with your binoculars you may see the heads of turkeys above the grass and brush. The wild turkey was reintroduced in Massachusetts in the 1970's after a hundred-year absence, and has made a remarkable comeback. They are much quicker than the farm-bred variety and can run through undergrowth as well as fly. Acorns, seeds and insects are among the turkey's favorite foods.

Ruffed grouse prefer the cover of woods or overgrown pastures and are easily flushed out if you walk by. The whirl of their wings startles even veteran hikers. This drumming sound is made by the male, who rapidly beats the air with his wings which produces an accelerating hollow roll. The drumming is used to attract females.

Bird Trends

In the last 35 years, the Quabbin—and Massachusetts as a whole—have seen an increase in birds as the common loon, great blue heron, turkey vulture, osprey, northern goshawk, wild turkey, barn owl, and common raven. Authors Richard Veit and Wayne Petersen in *Birds of Massachusetts* report that there are a variety of reasons for the increase of these species, which include human intervention and the increase in southern species (perhaps as a result of global warming). Biologist Bill Davis of the Massachusetts Division of Fisheries and Wildlife points out that the first documentation of nesting ravens in Massachusetts occurred at the Quabbin in 1982. The ravens have since used multiple nesting sites including rock outcrops on Mount Lizzie, Den Hill (located east of the baffle dams) and along the Quabbin spillway.

Other birds such as the American bittern, northern harrier, whip-poor-will and bobolink, are declining as marshland and grasslands areas become developed, and with the destruction of tropical forests used by neo-tropical migrant species.

Ecologist and frequent Quabbin birder Jack Lash points out that the Quabbin plays an important role in offering a habitat for warblers, another declining bird group. "Warblers," says Lash, "are migratory songbirds that require large, contiguous forested acreage, such as the Quabbin Reservation. Nearly two decades of bird monitoring data indicate that as many as twenty species of migratory warblers pass through or breed at Quabbin. Most are insect eaters. Many are canopy feeders, making them a challenge to see."

Mammals

Deer and Moose

The Quabbin and its surrounding towns host a healthy population of deer. If you don't get lucky and actually see a deer, look for its heart-shaped hoof prints or its antler rubs on trees. These rubs are usually about a foot or two up the trunks of saplings, where the bucks mark their territory in the fall. Here, the bark will be completely rubbed off on one side. Also, be on the lookout for scrapes on the ground; these are bare patches made by bucks pawing away leaf litter from an overhanging limb during the breeding season.

Deer, like most wild animals, are most often seen at dawn and dusk. One

White-tailed deer often venture into fields at Quabbin.

The moose are back at Quabbin, and their population is on the rise. Gate 33 is one area where they have been seen.

trick for spotting a deer is to look for a horizontal line (the deer's back) in a forest of vertical lines (the trees.) Currently, there is controlled deer hunting at the Quabbin by permit only. Before hunting was permitted, deer were so numerous at the Quabbin (4 to 6 times the state average) that they were eating most of the seedlings of trees that would have been beneficial in protecting the watershed. These trees prevent erosion, filter out contaminants and reduce the impact of acid rain. Without new trees the forest would become thinner, with more grassy areas and more vulnerable to fire, insect infestation and disease. Among the best places to see deer at the Quabbin is the Quabbin Park section of the Reservation.

Moose are relative newcomers to the Quabbin, after being extirpated from Massachusetts during Colonial times through subsistence hunting and loss of habitat. Their dark coats make them difficult to see at dusk when they are active. But by scanning marshes during the day and evening you may be able to pick out their large shapes. I've yet to see a moose at the Quabbin, but I have seen their tracks. The rangers who patrol the reservoir have told me they occasionally see moose in all sections of the Quabbin, with the most sightings occurring in the northern end. Moose eat twigs, leaves and aquatic plants, and usually the best

A beaver was working on cutting down this tree and left a pile of chips.

chance for seeing one is in an open marsh where they come to feed late in the day. The moose population at the Quabbin is breeding and their numbers are increasing each year. Bill Davis recommends exploring the Gate 33 area and the entire northeast section for a potential moose sighting.

Beaver, Muskrat, Mink and Otter

Beaver are mainly seen at dawn and dusk when they are repairing their dams, or cutting trees or saplings for food. Even if you don't see a beaver, chances are excellent you will find evidence of their presence at the Quabbin. Wood chips litter the ground next to pointed tree stumps with chisel-like tooth marks from the beaver's incisors. Scent mounds with mud and leaves near the water's edge mark beaver territory, along with well-defined trails and food caches.

Muskrat tend to stay in shallow wetlands rather than the main body of the reservoir. Muskrat are primarily vegetarians, eating aquatic plants and building igloo-shaped lodges out of plants and mud. (A beaver's lodge, by contrast, is much larger and includes bigger branches.)

Mink and otter are found along the edge of the reservoir, as well as marshes and rivers. Mink often prowl the shore in search of prey that includes snakes, frogs, birds, crayfish, and insects. They will also occasionally eat a muskrat. Your best chance of seeing a mink is at the edge of the reservoir or along a stream or marsh.

Most of my otter sightings have been during the winter.

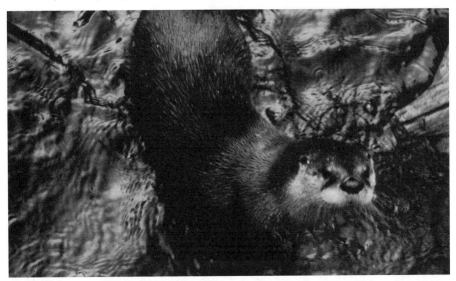

Otters spend most of their time in the water, and I've seen several at the Quabbin, particularly in the winter when they are prowling or swimming along the edge of open water and ice. Besides fish, otters eat crayfish, turtles and frogs. They are tremendous swimmers and have webbed feet. If you think you have come across otter tracks (the front track is about three inches long and the rear is about three-and-a-half inches long) a sure way to confirm your finding is a tail drag. Otters are quite large, weighing in the vicinity of fifteen to thirty pounds and measuring approximately four feet in length including the tail. Otters also love to slide, and these slides can be seen going down hills into the water. They can also be seen on snowy level areas, because an otter will run a few steps then slide through the snow. Otter "latrines" composed of piles of indigestible fish scales are often found along stream banks.

Porcupine and Fisher

Porcupines will eat the bark and buds off trees, preferring hemlocks above all others. Look for stunted hemlocks with ragged tops, or examine the forest floor below hemlock trees for recently nipped branches. Porcupine trails will often lead from a hemlock grove to a denning sight that is usually located in a miniature cave in a rocky outcrop. Such outcrops can be found in a number of areas within the Quabbin including Rattlesnake Hill at Gate 29. The porcupine population is kept in balance by their main predator, the fisher.

Porcupine will eat the buds of maple trees, but their favorite feeding tree is the hemlock.

Fishers are relative newcomers to the Quabbin after an absence of many years due to habitat changes (including loss of forest to farmland) and over-trapping. Now that forest has been reestablished in much of the Quabbin region, the fishers are back. Fishers are members of the weasel family and look similar to minks and martins. They are about the size of a large house cat, with dark brown fur and short legs. Their head is wedge-shaped and their ears are broad and rounded. Fishers can move quickly along the ground and also climb trees. They avoid man, so most sightings are purely by luck. You can, however, look for their tracks, which frequently lead to stumps and stone walls where they search for squirrels and chipmunks to hunt.

Fishers feed on mice, squirrels, rabbits, birds, frogs, insects, and supplement this meat diet with berries and apples. They also occasionally prey on the porcupine. The fisher is able to kill a porcupine by circling it and nipping at its head. This tires the porcupine and eventually it passes out from loss of blood.

I was once hiking near the Quabbin with noted wildlife photographer and tracker Paul Rezendes when we found several porcupine dens in rocky crevices. Paul then pointed out some tracks that were not those of the porcupine, and he explained they were made by a fisher. "The predator," Paul said, "has come for the prey."

Fox, Coyote and Bear

Fox can be seen hunting fields for mice and insects. In the spring the female has her litter in a den, usually identified by a large mound of dirt at its opening where the young kits will later play and sun themselves. Massachusetts has both red fox and gray fox, although the kind you are likely to see at the Quabbin is the red fox. Unlike the red fox, the gray fox can climb trees

Coyotes are well established at the Quabbin and it is not uncommon to see one. They look like small German shepards and usually have gray fur. I once saw ten coyotes crossing the ice in a single file, heading out to the carcass of a deer that eagles were feeding on. Coyotes eat just about anything they can catch but primarily focus on mice, rabbits, small game and weak or injured deer. The owner of Brookfield Orchards told me when he mows his fields, coyotes sometimes follow behind him, pouncing on the exposed mice in the cut grass.

Some of my best viewing of coyotes and foxes has come not while walking the Quabbin but during my drives on nearby back roads. Oftentimes wildlife will not flee from cars, so if you have your camera ready you may get a great shot. Just be sure to take the photo from your car after you have carefully rolled down your window, because once an animal hears the click of a car door opening it will usually vanish.

Black bears have been seen at the Quabbin but it is uncertain whether or not there is a breeding population. The black bear population in Massachusetts has been expanding in recent years, but most of the bears are located west of

Red fox kits enjoy the sun on a mound of dirt outside their den.

the Connecticut River. Black bears usually avoid humans unless they are purposely being fed. Chances are, if you are lucky enough to see one in the woods, you will only see its hind end as it runs for cover. A female bear with cubs, however, is not to be trifled with, and if you come upon one freeze and then very slowly walk away.

The Mystery of the Mountain Lion

There has been no definitive proof that mountain lions (cougars) are living in Massachusetts, but there have been plenty of unsubstantiated sightings in the greater Quabbin area. While most of the mountain lion sightings can probably be attributed to misidentification of other predators, such as bobcat or coyote, I'm of the opinion it's possible one or two could roam the Quabbin. One ranger at the Quabbin said he has never seen a mountain lion in all his years of patrolling, but he thinks it's possible that one or two might live there. He thought this would have been especially true a few years back when the deer population was at its peak.

John McCarter, a wildlife tracker who often works with Paul Rezendes, thinks there is a mountain lion at the Quabbin. He has discovered scat he believes to be from a mountain lion and a cache of food that has mountain lion characteristics. Analysis was done on the scat by two different labs; and one lab found no evidence of mountain lion fur but the other determined by DNA testing that it was cougar scat. Some biologists are convinced that McCarter's find was from a mountain lion but think it may have been from an illegally released cougar, because no additional hard evidence has been found.

Over the years I've met several people who have told me they've seen a mountain lion at the Quabbin or in nearby towns. Bob Clark, president of the Friends of Quabbin and a frequent hiker, has seen two mountain lions over several years, both on the east side of Quabbin. Jack Swedberg also saw a mountain lion at Quabbin in the 1960's.

If mountain lions are reestablished at the Quabbin it will be a noteworthy occurrence, as the last known recorded sighting of a mountain lion in Massachusetts was in Hampshire County in 1858.

Biking and Back Roads

The following routes can be explored by bicycle or car. Most are loops along back roads, but I encourage you to venture off the loops to discover the joys of finding new places off the beaten track. The distances are not especially long, so if you are traveling by car, or you want to extend your bike trip, you may want to follow multiple loops as part of the same trip. You may want to review the hiking section of this book to combine your back-roading adventure with a walk in the woods.

New Salem & Orange
Lake Mattawa, the Bear's Den, and the Hessian Soldiers

This route starts at the intersection of Elm Street and Neilson Road in New Salem, and winds through the surrounding hills in a circle, covering a distance of about seven miles and passing several interesting points along the way. The route only follows back roads where cars are scarce.

Follow Neilson Road half a mile and be on the lookout for the little sign for the Bear's Den waterfall where there is parking for several cars on the right-hand side of the road. In the summer the falls are normally just a trickle, but in the spring the river flexes its muscles and water cascades over each side of a giant boulder. The shiny evergreen leaves of mountain laurel growing beneath enormous hemlocks twinkle on sunny days. There is also a tiny cave and evidence of a millsite.

Legend has it that Metacom, also known King Philip, camped here, planning his raids on Hatfield and Deerfield during King Philip's War. But like the saying, "George Washington slept here," Metacom is said to have been everywhere, and over time his legend grows.

After exploring the Bear's Den, continue up Neilson Road another mile and turn right onto Crowl Road. Crowl Road is a well-maintained dirt road that passes through a stately line of sugar maples and old farmland in the process of reverting back to forest.

New Salem & Orange

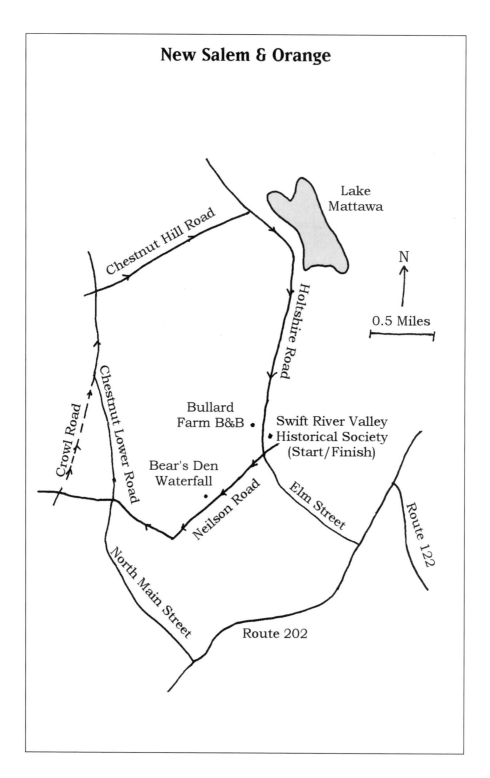

Lake Mattawa

Chestnut Hill Road

Holtshire Road

N

0.5 Miles

Crowl Road

Chestnut Lower Road

Bullard Farm B&B

Swift River Valley Historical Society (Start/Finish)

Bear's Den Waterfall

Neilson Road

Elm Street

Route 122

North Main Street

Route 202

Crowl Road passes out of New Salem and into Orange. After 1.4 miles you'll reach an intersection where you should turn left on Chestnut Hill Lower Road, which is paved. Proceed about a half-mile and turn right on Chestnut Hill Road, gliding downhill for a half-mile to the intersection with Holtshire Road. At this point, Lake Mattawa, which features good trout fishing, will be in front of you. Turn right on Holtshire Road, and travel along the edge of the lake, traveling back into New Salem. In two miles you will have just about completed your loop, passing by Bullard Farm then onward to the Swift River Valley Historical Society buildings (open seasonally). Look carefully across the street from the historical society for a small granite marker recalling a bit of history from the Revolutionary War. The marker reads, "October, 25, 1777. 1,000 Hessians who surrendered at Saratoga passed here."

There is also an interesting signpost by the historical society's barn, with arrows pointing the way to the four towns that were drowned by the Quabbin. This single signpost stood at five different corner locations in New Salem during the 1800's and 1900's. One arrow oddly points the way to "Indianapolis," but my biking legs are not quite in shape to tackle that 900-mile ride!

Shutesbury and Leverett
A Gloomy Ride Through Rattlesnake Gutter Road Into Beautiful North Leverett
This route covers approximately 15 miles with a few gradual hills and a couple of steep hills. (Note: Part of Rattlesnake Gutter Road is closed in the winter.)

An old mill at north Leverett.

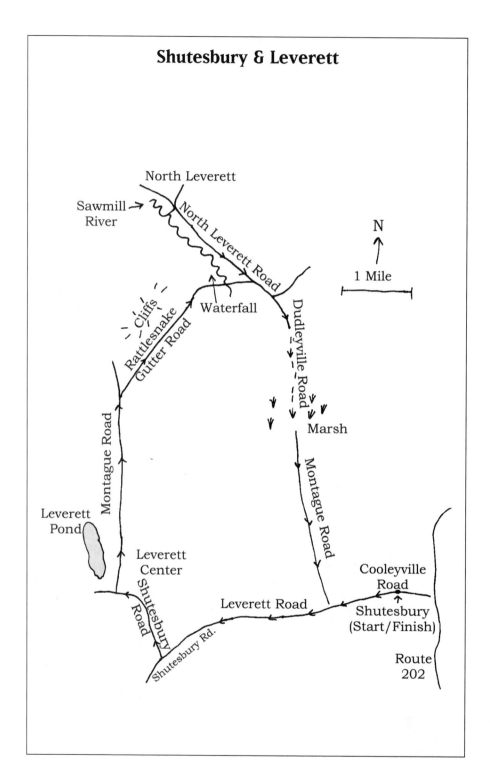

Shutesbury & Leverett

North Leverett

Sawmill River

North Leverett Road

N

1 Mile

Cliffs

Rattlesnake Gutter Road

Waterfall

Dudleyville Road

Montague Road

Marsh

Montague Road

Leverett Pond

Leverett Center

Shutesbury Road

Shutesbury Rd.

Leverett Road

Cooleyville Road

Shutesbury (Start/Finish)

Route 202

Begin your ride from the little hilltop town green of Shutesbury, located about a mile from Route 202. (A sign on Route 202 directs you to the green.) From the green proceed west on Coolyville Road which turns into Leverett Road. The ride is mostly downhill, and parallels a brook as you leave Shutesbury and enter Leverett. There are a few homes, but most of the time you will pass through forest.

After traveling about four miles you will reach a "T" intersection where you should turn right on Shutesbury Road, heading toward Leverett Center. At 1.5 miles you will reach Leverett Pond, where you can walk down to the water and see red-wing blackbirds and ducks in the spring. Turn right at the pond and follow Montague Road, passing the old town hall and a church. Go 1.8 mile to one of my favorite roads, Rattlesnake Gutter Road, where the road is as eerie as its name. Turn right onto Rattlesnake Gutter Road. You will pass by a couple of beautifully landscaped homes before entering the darkness of a hemlock forest.

It's easy to imagine that there were once rattlers in the rocky crags in the forest along Rattlesnake Gutter Road, and perhaps there still are. (Timber rattlesnakes are a protected, endangered species in Massachusetts.) There are precipitous drops on the left side of the road, where there is a ravine filled with large boulders. The rocks form little caves, and this is a good spot to find a porcupine denning in one of these caves or munching on the needles of a hemlock tree.

Where the granite ledge rises 80 feet above the road, I decided to investigate this mysterious place on foot. Using my hands to grip the rocks I slowly traversed along a ledge of earth, but found myself continually glancing around me, thinking a rattler was coiled on the granite outcrops. "What a strange place," I thought. "Why did someone bother to build a road through here," I wondered. I also wondered how the ravine formed, since there was no river at the bottom, just a jumble of forbidding rocks.

I didn't get far with my rock climbing, so I worked my way back to my bike. Rattlesnake Gutter Road is only about a mile and a half long, before it reaches the Saw Mill River at a waterfall. From here you can sidetrack to the village of North Leverett by turning left on North Leverett Road and proceeding northwest for half a mile. This little village is quite handsome, complete with an old sawmill perched above the river at another waterfall. Most of our smallmills have long since disappeared, but this one is typical of the type of building that was erected along almost every brook and river in Massachusetts before the 1900's.

To continue the loop ride and head back to your car, return to the end of Rattlesnake Gutter Road by the first waterfall and proceed straight past the river for less than half a mile to the intersection with Dudleyville Road. By bearing right on Dudleyville Road, which turns into a dirt road, you will be heading back toward Shutesbury Center. Dudleyville Road becomes Montague Road, passing a marsh where you might see a wood duck or maybe even a moose. It's about four miles back to Leverett Road, where you turn left and travel about a mile to reach the Shutesbury town common.

A Petersham Loop

Old Millstones on the East Branch and a House Turned Backward

This ride through Petersham is a short loopof just six miles, but bicyclists will be challenged by moderate hills, and those traveling in cars will have many points of interest deserving of a stop and exploration on foot. Be sure to bring your camera!

From the Country Store in Petersham center, follow East Street which starts at the side of the Country Store and heads downhill past fields, homes and an old mill site complete with millstone and waterfall. About a mile and half down East Street you will pass a handsome cemetery with three huge maples, followed by a private road on the left leading uphill through long lines of maples to a farm. This road is appropriately called Maple Lane. After two miles take a right onto Quaker Road. You will pass over a swiftly moving stream, followed by an old stone foundation standing eight to 12 feet tall and partially hidden in the woods on the left. At the intersection with Hall Road on your left you should bear right, continuing on Quaker Road. You will then proceed through a forest before passing over the East Branch of the Swift River. After about two miles, Quaker Road ends at Route 32. Turn right on Route 32, heading north toward Petersham center.

As you approach the intersection of Routes 122 and 32 (at South Street) take a careful look at a two-story white house on your left. This house was turned around to spite the town in 1886. The front door once faced the intersection of the main roads, but an angry owner named Forester Goddard jacked up the house and turned it around so its back presently faces the town center. Goddard had been hired by the town to repair a stone wall in the village cemetery. Repairing this wall cost more than the town had anticipated and a disagreement arose over what would be a fair price to compensate Goddard. When the town ultimately refused to pay Goddard's price, he decided to show his contempt for the town officials. Goddard jacked up his house, put croquet balls under the

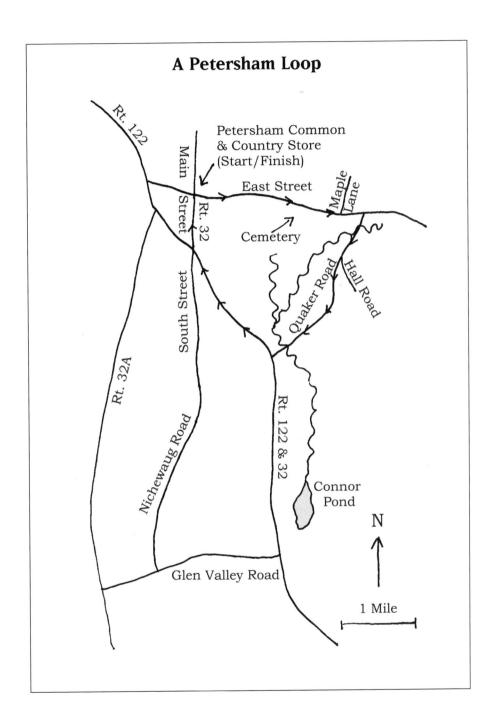

A Petersham Loop

Rt. 122

Main Street

Petersham Common
& Country Store
(Start/Finish)

East Street

Maple Lane

Rt. 32

Cemetery

Quaker Road

Hall Road

South Street

Rt. 32A

Nichewaug Road

Rt. 122 & 32

Connor Pond

N

Glen Valley Road

1 Mile

structure at various intervals, and with the aid of his wife inched the house around so that the front faced southward toward his fields, and the house's backside faced the town center. More than a century later the house still expresses the mason's contempt for Petersham.

Continue your ride to the Petersham common and the Country Store, where you can reward yourself with a cold drink and a slice of pie.

For a longer ride, try riding from Petersham to Barre. From the Country Store follow East Street, and instead of turning onto Quaker Road, continue straight. East Street turns into Old Barre Road, which leads past rolling meadows, marsh and woods before eventually bringing you to the center of Barre.

Another Petersham Loop
Along the Swift River Reservation

This loop of about nine miles is mostly to the west of Petersham center, as opposed to the initial ride which was to the east.

Begin your outing from Petersham center and go south on Route 32 for about a half-mile. Cross where Route 32 intersects with Route 122, and go straight on South Street. Follow South Street about a mile to Nichewaug Road, and continue going south another mile and a half to the intersection with Glen Valley Road and turn right. This is a narrow lane that cuts though a beautiful hemlock forest, following the rushing waters of the East Branch of the Swift River. Much of the land here is owned by the Trustees of Reservations and by Harvard University, and is excellent for hiking. Continue about a mile to the intersection with Route 32A, where you should turn right. You are now heading north, and you should follow Route 32A about three miles to where it joins Route 122, and continue north a short distance until you take a right on West Street. West Street will bring you past some fine old homes and then back to Petersham center.

Hardwick Loop
Hilltop Countryside

This ride begins and ends in the center of Hardwick, covering five-and-a-half miles of country roads. From Hardwick center, go north on Route 32A about .4 mile then turn right on North Street. North Street turns into Spring Hill Lane, which runs along a ridge passing by some scenic farms. At the end of Spring Hill Lane turn left onto Old Dana Road which turns into Barre-Dana Road, and follow this to its end where you should turn left on Route 32A (south) which will bring you back to Hardwick center.

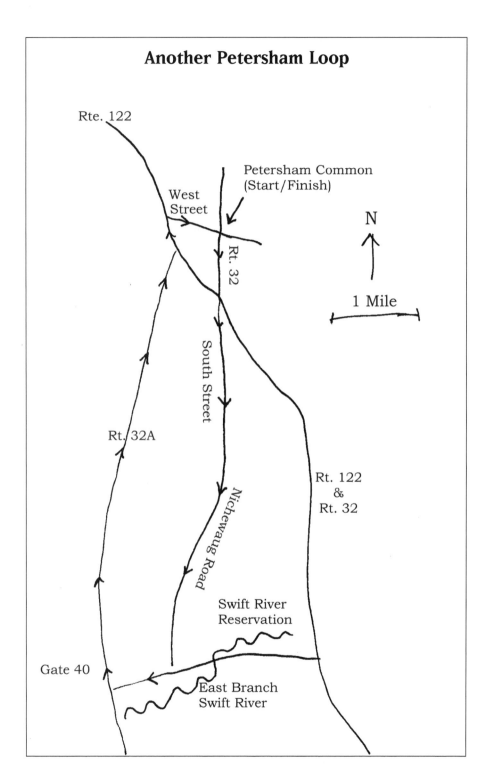

Another Petersham Loop

Rte. 122

Petersham Common
(Start/Finish)

West
Street

Rt. 32

N

1 Mile

South Street

Rt. 32A

Nichewaug Road

Rt. 122
&
Rt. 32

Swift River
Reservation

Gate 40

East Branch
Swift River

West Brookfield, New Braintree, and Hardwick

Riding Through History

When I am back roading, the criteria I look for are peaceful country lanes, great scenery, and plenty of history. This ramble has all three. Particularly important to bicyclists is that this long loop trip brings you back to your starting point. Total estimated distance is 18 miles, but there are plenty of great resting spots, and it is easy to plan a shorter trip. Because of its length and the hills along the route, this ride is perhaps better suited for driving than biking but experienced bikers may want to give it a try. If you are uncertain about your ability to bike the complete distance, you may want to leave your car near the Clover Hill Country Store at the intersection of Hardwick Road and Route 32, and bike a portion of the route.

The ride begins at the town line between Brookfield and West Brookfield at Foster Hill-Old West Brookfield Road, which runs off Route 9. (The eastern section of the road in Brookfield is called Old West Brookfield Road, and the western part of the road is called Foster Hill.) There's enough history and scenic beauty on this one road to please every explorer.

The eastern part of the road at the start of the route has a hill that keeps bicyclist's speeds down, which is a good thing because partially hidden in the grass on the right side of the road is a Benjamin Franklin milestone. This milestone is located across the street from a brown house and is about 300 yards east of the garrison site described in the next paragraph. The tombstone-shaped rock has an inscription on it that reads, "67 miles to Boston, 36 miles to Springfield." The milestone is said to have been placed here by Benjamin Franklin (or one of his assistants) when postage was paid by the mile.

About 300 yards west of the milestone is the site of the Brookfield garrison that was attacked by Nipmuck warriors during King Philip's War. The raid occurred in 1675 when the Nipmucks ambushed Captain Wheeler and Captain Hutchinson, then burned the town of Brookfield before laying siege to the garrison. (See the "Nipmuck Warriors and the Seige of Brookfield" chapter in the "Forgotten History of the Region" section of this book for more information.) A large stone marker indicates the site of the garrison, and there is a beautiful etching depicting the Indians pushing a burning wagon of hay toward the garrison. Luckily for the settlers and the surviving soldiers who were trapped inside the garrison, the skies opened up and a deluge of rain put out the fire. Soon thereafter reinforcements arrived and the Nipmucks reluctantly retreated back to their village on the Ware River.

It seems each time I ramble through Brookfield something new catches my

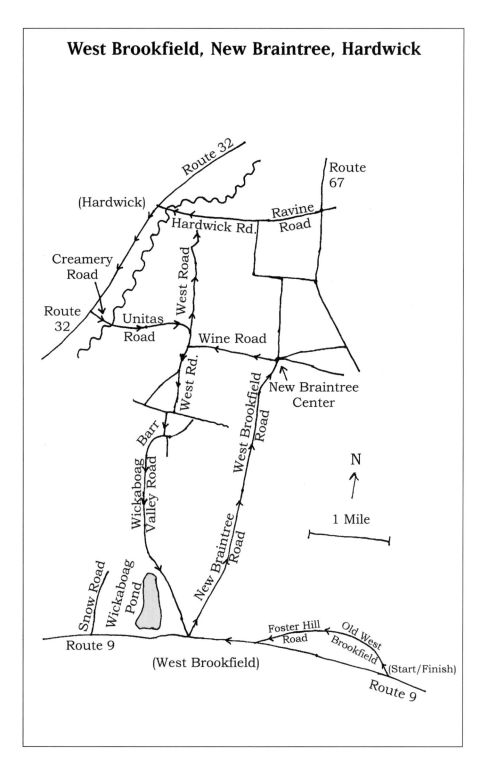

West Brookfield, New Braintree, Hardwick

Route 32

(Hardwick)

Route 67

Hardwick Rd.

Ravine Road

Creamery Road

West Road

Route 32

Unitas Road

Wine Road

West Rd.

New Braintree Center

Barr

N

West Brookfield Road

Wickaboag Valley Road

1 Mile

Snow Road

Wickaboag Pond

New Braintree Road

Route 9

(West Brookfield)

Foster Hill Road

Old West Brookfield

(Start/Finish)

Route 9

eye. On a recent excursion with my dad, he spotted a huge rock with a plaque on it. The rock was set back in a field on Foster Hill Road about a quarter-mile west of the garrison site on the north side of the road. We climbed over a stone wall and walked through a field of Queen Anne's lace and the purple flowers of blooming clover. The plaque commemorated a Reverend Whitefield. When I first saw the rock I had no idea who Whitefield was, but as I stood looking at the name, I realized I'd recently come across it. Strangely enough, the book I had been reading, which mentioned Whitefield, was written by another man who is famous on this road, Benjamin Franklin. Even more curious is the fact that the two men never crossed paths in Massachusetts, but instead met in Philadelphia. What are the odds that two stones, hidden in the woods on the same road, have such a connection? Equally odd is that on the day my father discovered the Whitefield Rock, I'd given him Benjamin Franklin's autobiography to read. This is the reason why the Whitefield name rang a bell with me.

Franklin observed that Whitefield was a remarkable itinerant preacher who was not allowed by the clergy to speak in their churches. Whitefield, however, was not deterred. He simply spoke in the open fields where the common folk gathered 'round. Franklin wrote, "Multitudes of all sects and denominations attended his sermons, and greatly admired him, not withstanding his common abuse of them. He assured them they were naturally half beasts and half devils, and it was wonderful to see the change this soon made in the manners of our inhabitants. From being thoughtless about religion, it seemed as if all the world were growing religious; so that one could not walk through the town in an evening without hearing psalms sung in different families of every street."

Whitefield preached from New England to Georgia. While in the South he came across many homeless children whose parents had died while toiling to clear the land. Whitefield made it his mission to build an orphanage for these children and traveled through the North successfully collecting money for his project. He must have had considerable charisma along with his significant oratory skills, as people filled the streets and fields to hear him, and were absolutely silent while he spoke.

Continuing to the end of Foster Hill Road, turn right onto Route 9 for a short distance and then right onto New Braintree Road. After leaving a residential area, the road will take you through a wooded area with an occasional cornfield. About three miles up New Braintree Road you'll arrive at the tiny center of New Braintree, with its post office, church and Kip's Tree Farm. (Look for the reindeer behind the barn at Kip's.)

Turn left here onto Wine Road and cruise downhill about a mile and a half, passing fields of blueberries, then turn right on West Road. Another stone marker is hidden on West Road on the right-hand side, designating the site where the Nipmucks ambushed the soldiers before the attack on Brookfield. (Historians have searched for the exact spot of this deadly ambush, referred to as "Wheeler's' Surprise," but there has never been a conclusive finding.)

West Road offers plenty of scenic views, and after a mile and a half it will bring you to Hardwick Road. Turn left here and cross the Ware River to Route 32. Turn left onto Route 32 heading south. Just a hundred feet up the road on the right you can stop for a snack at the Clover Hill Country Store.

If you continue along the loop back to West Brookfield, be alert, as the roads are not well marked. To return to West Brookfield center, follow Route 32 southward two miles, then turn left onto Creamery Road. Follow Creamery Road over the Ware River where it soon turns into Unitas Road, and continue up the hills for a couple of miles to the intersection with West Road. Turn right onto West Road and go about two miles to its end. Then turn right after about a hundred feet, and take a left onto Barr Road, passing over a stream by a farm. (One of the oldest white oak trees in the country is located not too far away. For directions see "The New Braintree White Oak" in the chapter "Nearby Hikes.")

To return to the West Brookfield town common follow Barr Road which turns into Wickaboag Road and brings you back to the town common after traveling six miles.

(For a future exploration trip to West Brookfield, check out Snow Road just east of the Salem Cross Inn on Route 9. Snow Road has a handsome farm situated on the left side of the road with over a mile of white fencing separating a network of pastures. Bring your camera.)

Warren/West Brookfield

Lucy Stone and Quaboag River

This 9.5-mile ride is suitable for summer and fall only, as some of the roads are dirt (muddy in the spring and slippery in winter). The ride begins at the intersection of Route 9 and Coy Hill Road at the western end of West Brookfield. Proceed up Coy Hill Road about .4 mile and you will pass the Lucy Stone Birthplace granite marker and sign. Lucy Stone was the first woman in Massachusetts to graduate from college. She put her education to good use, crusading for women's rights at a time when they could not vote. Although largely overlooked by history, Lucy Stone was ahead of her time, devoting her life to equality for all people.

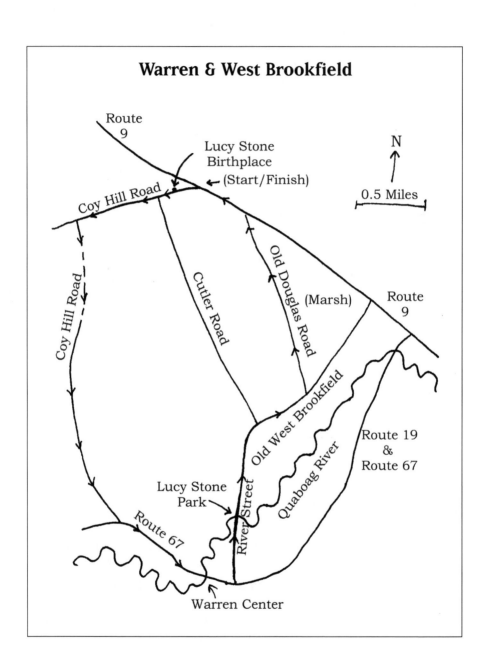

Warren & West Brookfield

Route 9

Lucy Stone Birthplace
(Start/Finish)

N

0.5 Miles

Coy Hill Road

Coy Hill Road

Cutler Road

Old Douglas Road

(Marsh)

Route 9

Old West Brookfield

Quaboag River

Route 19
&
Route 67

Lucy Stone Park

River Street

Route 67

Warren Center

Coy Hill Road is a narrow, rugged country lane, shaded by large oaks and maples. Where the road forks, stay to the left on Coy Hill Road which now becomes a dirt road. Climb a moderate hill and after 1.2 miles, bear left, again staying on Coy Hill Road, passing a radio tower. The road becomes paved again, passing through cornfields with some nice views to the southeast. Here you start your descent into Warren for a couple more miles until you reach Route 67. Turn left on Route 67, following the Quaboag River into the center of Warren where you can stop for a snack. About .8 miles down Route 67, just after you cross the river, turn left onto River Street which becomes Old West Brookfield Road. About a half-mile up the road is a pleasant little park along the banks of the Quaboag River, appropriately named Lucy Stone Park, indicating that the locals have not forgotten this remarkable woman. Proceed up Old West Brookfield Road another mile and a half and bear left onto Old Douglas Road. It's a good road for wildlife viewing, passing along the edge of a marsh and through an oak forest before bringing you back to Route 9 after a couple of miles. Turn left and in .3 mile you will be back at the intersection of Coy Hill Road.

New Braintree and Hardwick
A Ware River Ramble

This 9 to ten mile ride starts at Reed's Country Store on Route 67 in New Braintree. (Before this ride you may want to stop at Reed's Country Store and pick up some supplies for a picnic at the halfway point.) From Reed's follow Oakham Road about a mile west to the tiny center of New Braintree which is comprised of a church, a post office, Kip's Tree Farm, and an old cemetery. Travel northwest on Wine Road, which is very hilly but fortunately mainly downhill in this direction. At the end of Wine Road (about a mile from New Braintree center), turn right and follow West Road for just 0.2 mile and then turn left onto Unitas Road which travels mainly through a wooded area. After about a mile and a half, Unitas Road crosses the Ware River where you may want to do some exploring on foot, or perhaps even fish since trout are stocked here. The Ware River can also be canoed, although in the summer it may be a little shallow. Just across the river, Unitas Road turns into Creamery Road and ends at Route 32. Turn right on Route 32 and follow the Ware River northward about 1.8 miles to Hardwick Road on the right. The Old Furnace Canoe Launch and Park is located here, a perfect spot for a picnic.

Follow Hardwick Road eastward through the open fields by the river. This is the area where the Nipmuck Indians had their huge Wennimessit village, and there is a granite marker on the left side of the road indicating that King Philip

New Braintree & Hardwick

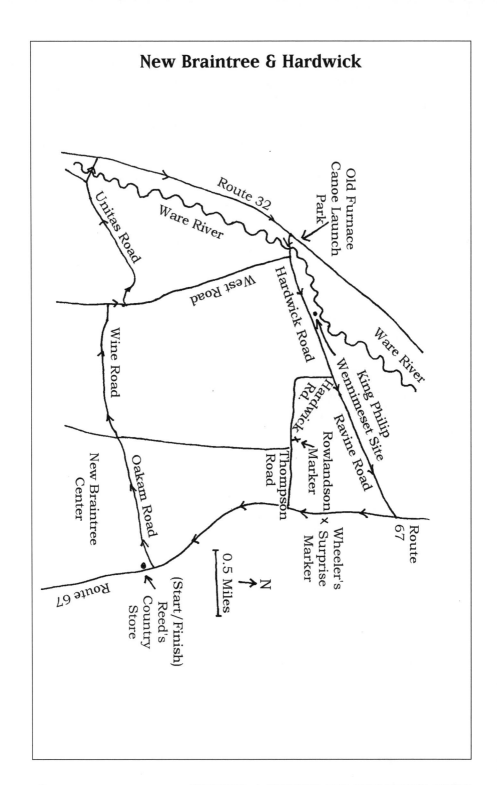

stopped here. Hardwick Road turns into Ravine Road and you should follow these roads about two and a half miles to the junction of Route 67. Turn right on Route 67 heading south, past the sign for the "Wheelers Surprise" ambush site, and back to Reed's which is about two miles down the road. (If you want to see the marker where Mary Rowlandson's daughter, Sarah, died while being held captive by Nipmucks during King Philip's War, turn right onto Thompson Road just after the "Wheeler's Surprise" sign. Follow Thompson Road past Hardwick Road on the left, and the stone marker is just a few feet beyond the intersection on the right side. See the "Nipmuck Warriors and the Seige of Brookfield.")

Hardwick Common is the sight of an agricultural fair each August.

QUABBIN: A HISTORY AND EXPLORER'S GUIDE

A Trip to Sturbridge

Sturbridge is closer to the Quabbin than many travelers realize. You need not travel on the Massachusetts Turnpike if you're coming from the Quabbin area, but instead take Route 9 into Brookfield and then head south on Route 148 into Sturbridge. It's a side trip worth taking, because Sturbridge is not only home to the well-known Old Sturbridge Village, but several other interesting destinations as well. And while many of the shops, antique stores, hotels and restaurants are on Route 20, there are quiet back roads heading into the countryside.

Old Sturbridge Village

Old Sturbridge Village is an outdoor living history museum that tells the story of everyday life in a small New England town during the years from 1790 to 1840. Because no cars are allowed in Old Sturbridge Village, visitors really feel as if they are entering a bygone time. Surrounding the common is a bank, a general store, a law office, craft shops and homes. Many of the original buildings from the early 1800's were brought here from other parts of New England. Side paths lead to a blacksmith shop and cooper shop as well as a woolen mill, sawmill and a gristmill operated by water power. From the village green visitors can walk to a working 19th century farm where the tools and skills of the period are put to use in the surrounding hayfields, orchards, gardens, and pastures. In addition to the re-created historical community, a museum displays exhibits that include a collection of New England glass, firearms and military accoutrements, lighting devices, and an outstanding collection of regional clocks. Just outside the museum is a colorful, aromatic herb garden

Unlike a traditional museum, Old Sturbridge Village is alive with craftsmen and women who demonstrate such forgotten tasks as shaping horseshoes, printing newspaper from a 200-year-old printing press, weaving and spinning, candle dipping, cobbling, and cooking over an open hearth. You can chat with these workers, discuss religion with a period preacher, or learn what subjects were taught in a rural school that served all ages. Handsome gardens adorn the prop-

Greater Sturbridge & Brookfield

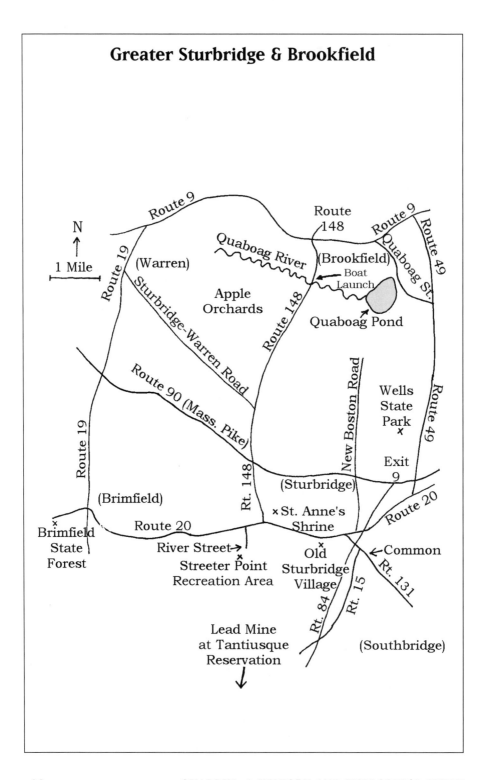

N

1 Mile

Route 9

Route 148

Route 9

Route 49

Route 19

(Warren)

Quaboag River

(Brookfield)

Quaboag St.

Boat Launch

Apple Orchards

Route 148

Quaboag Pond

Sturbridge-Warren Road

Route 90 (Mass. Pike)

New Boston Road

Wells State Park

Route 49

Route 19

Rt. 148

Exit 9

(Sturbridge)

(Brimfield)

× St. Anne's Shrine

Route 20

Brimfield State Forest

Route 20

Common

Rt. 131

River Street →

Streeter Point Recreation Area

Old Sturbridge Village

Rt. 84

Rt. 15

Lead Mine at Tantiusque Reservation

(Southbridge)

erty; and horses, oxen and other animals employed in farming and transportation are scattered about. All this historic activity makes Old Sturbridge Village a big hit with both children and adults.

The early 1800's were a time of great change in New England, particularly with the rapid growth in the 1830's of the mechanized textile industry. Mechanization led to a proliferation of water-powered spinning and weaving factories that lured thousands of people off the farm and into the factories. New markets were expanding at the same time due to the settlement of the west and

Gathering apples for cider at Old Sturbridge Village. (Photo by Thomas Neill, courtesy of Old Sturbridge Village.)

population increases in American cities along the eastern seaboard. Transportation improvements also caused trade to boom as thousands of miles of turnpikes, railroads, and canals were built across the country. Old Sturbridge Village captures this period of change when some households abandoned subsistence farming in exchange for factory wages. As you walk from the quiet pastures of the Freeman Farm to the Carding Mill with its early machinery advances, it's as if you are passing from one era into the beginning of another.

Seasonal events include maple sugaring, an old-fashioned Fourth of July celebration, harvest weekends, and a special Thanksgiving event. For admission hours it's best to call ahead (508-347-3362), because Old Sturbridge Village has different schedules depending upon the month. The only time that the village is closed on weekdays is from January 2 to February 17, when it is only open on weekends. The rest of the year it is open either daily, or daily except Mondays.

OTHER POINTS OF INTEREST IN STURBRIDGE

Tantiusques Reservation

Owned by The Trustees of Reservations, the Tantiusques Reservation is one of the few places in Massachusetts where you can see an old graphite mine. Although the mine's opening is only about four feet by four feet, it extends back about forty feet into the rock ledge. The Nipmuck Indians were the first to excavate graphite, or "black lead," using it to paint their faces for tribal ceremonies. Later, John Winthrop purchased this land in 1644, writing to his son, "There is some black lead digged, but not so much as they expected it being very difficult to gett out of ye rocks...." Winthrop's efforts commenced many years of commercial mining here. Some years were profitable, but in most years the results were similar to what Winthrop described in his letter. By the mid-1800's, the graphite was being packed into barrels and hauled to Boston by horse-drawn carts, where it was then shipped to London.

There are several mining cuts in the rock in addition to the small tunnel. In winter, unusual ice formations hang from the cuts and the cliffs and make for interesting photographs. One winter, the tunnel had stalagmites of ice rising from the floor where drops of water had fallen from the ceiling. Winter is also the time to see the tracks of the deer, fox and coyote that live in these woods of oak and hemlock. (The hemlocks are currently under attack from a microscopic insect called the wooly adelgid. If the hemlock needles have a white coloration underneath, it's a sign of infestation.)

Strange ice formations inside a lead mine at Tauntiusques Reservation.

Besides the mining cuts and tunnel, the reservation has a 1.75-mile trail that leads through thick stands of mountain laurel. In the late spring the flower of the mountain laurel blooms, but the bushes are equally handsome in the winter when the sun, shining from its low, southern position, hits the waxy leaves of the plant making them twinkle above a snow-covered forest floor.

Directions: From I-84 west take Exit 1, Mashapaug Road-Southbridge. Turn right off the exit ramp and follow Route 15 south for 1.5 miles. Turn right onto Leadmine Road and travel 0.9 mile to the entrance on the left. (Open year-round; no admission fee; no restrooms.)

Sturbridge Common

Sturbridge common off Route 131 is a handsome village green with interesting side roads featuring homes from the 1820's and 1830's. The Joshua Hyde Library on the north side of the common is a good example of Greek Revival architecture. Just past the common, the yellow and red Hyde House is a blend of Gothic and Greek Revival styles. The area around the common is a great place to stretch your legs and visit antique shops, or stop for a bite to eat at the Publick House Historic Inn built in 1771. Telephone 508-347-3313.

Saint Anne Shrine

In the late 1800's a parishioner was healed of dropsy at this site on the Sunday following the feast of Saint Anne, and ever since believers think miracles continue to happen here. The property includes two churches, an outdoor Mass Pavilion, Way of the Cross, gift shop, statues and a collection of Russian icons. Located on Church Street, just west of Old Sturbridge Village off Route 20. Telephone 508-347-7338.

Hemlock Ridge Golf Course

Nine-hole course, carts available. Located on Holland Road. Telephone 508-347-9466.

Hyland Orchard and Brewery

Free brewery tours, samplings, picnic areas and animal attractions. Located at 199 Arnold Road, Sturbridge. Telephone 508-347-7500.

Stageloft Repertory Theater

Fine entertainment (seasonal). Located on Main Street, Sturbridge. Telephone 508-347-9005.

Wells State Park

Wells State Park features 1,500 acres of hilly woodland excellent for hiking, swamps, beaver flowages in the lowlands, and a lake for boating and fishing. There are 60 camping sites available with showers and restrooms. Located off Route 49 on Mountain Road. Telephone 508-347-9257.

Bethlehem in Sturbridge

Bethlehem in Sturbridge is located on the entrance road to Old Sturbridge Village. The museum displays depict the Biblical story of creation, the centuries before Christ's birth, His life and crucifixion. There is also a 50-foot diorama of Bethlehem as it was in Christ's time. The diorama includes animated figures such as horses and donkeys, and campfires that smoke. The museum also features articles from the Holy Land. It's best to call ahead for hours and performance times. Located in Sturbridge at 72 Stallion Hill. Telephone 508-347-3013.

Streeter Point Recreation Area

Located just off Route 20 near the Sturbridge/Brimfield line. Good for boating and fishing in Long Pond and East Brimfield Lake.

Westville Lake Recreation Area

Picnicing, fishing (trout, bass, pickerel), boating and athletic fields beside a 23-acre lake. Trout are stocked in the Quinebaug River above the dam. The Old Grand Trunk Railroad parallels the Quinebaug River and is a popular walking trail. Otters, deer, beaver and fox are frequently seen. The U.S. Army Corps of Engineers owns and manages the 578 acres at Westville Lake. The Westville Lake Dam provides flood control protection for communities along the Quinebaug River. Located on Wallace Road off Route 131 near the Southbridge line.

POINTS OF INTEREST NEAR STURBRIDGE

Capen Hill Nature Sanctuary

This is a good spot for the kids with pond, trails, natural history exhibits, and a wildlife rehabilitation facility. Located on Capen Hill Road off Route 20, Charlton. Telephone 508-248-5516.

Mellea Winery

Although the vineyards cover only three acres, the winery offers fascinating tours where viewers can not only see the wine-making process and hand-operated equipment, but also sample the wine itself. There is a nice picnic area by a pond. The Mellea Winery is located off Route 131 on Old Southbridge Road in West Dudley. Telephone 508-943-5166.

Quaboag River and Quaboag Wildlife Management Area

This area consists of a large marsh with the Quaboag River winding through it. There is access for canoes, kayaks and small boats on Route 148 in Brookfield and East Brookfield. (There are plans to open a canoe rental operation and café called White's Landing, located where the river crosses Route 148.) The river spreads through extensive marshland which is a nesting area for the American bittern. These rare birds disguise themselves by "freezing" with their necks up so they blend into the surrounding cattails. You can identify them by their call, which sounds like a throaty "oonk-a-lunk." Northern pike abound in the river, and spawn in its shallows just after ice-out. The section of the river near Route 148 is flat water, but in Warren to the west, there are rapids.

East Brimfield Lake/Holland Pond

These bodies of water offer swimming, boating, fishing and hiking. The Quinebaug River presents a seven-mile flat-water canoe trail through broad wetlands and forest. There are no portages on the entire seven miles. Wildlife includes painted turtles, water snakes, red-winged blackbirds, beaver, great blue heron, mink, otters and frogs. Holland Pond is at the southern end of the U.S. Army Corps of Engineers property and can be accessed off Holland/East Brimfield Road which runs from Route 20 in Sturbridge south to Holland, where you will see signs for the park and an access road called Morse Road. East Brimfield Lake is stocked with trout. The Quinebaug River flows from Holland Pond to East Brimfield Lake. Access to East Brimfield Lake is via the Streeter Recreation Area off Route 20 on the Sturbridge/Brimfield line. For more information telephone the U.S. Army Corps of Engineers at 508-347-3705.

Grizzly Adams Grave
This is the burial site of John Capen "Grizzly" Adams, the 19th century animal trainer. The headstone was commissioned by his friend, P.T. Barnum. Located at Bay Path Cemetery, Route 31, Charlton.

Brimfield Flea Market
Brimfield is a short drive from Sturbridge and is known for the huge Brimfield Flea Market and Antique Show held along Route 20. Just about everything and anything is available for sale here with vendors from across America. Telephone 413-245-7479.

Brimfield State Forest
The Brimfield State Forest is a 3,250-acre forest with swimming, hiking, fishing, and picnicking. It is located on Dearth Hill Road off Route 20 in Brimfield. Telephone Wells State Park for information, 508-347-9257.

The Arts Center
Art shows, exhibitions, concerts, workshops and demonstrations are featured in a restored Victorian mansion and carriage house. The Gateway Players, the area's oldest resident community theatre group, uses this as their home base. Located at 111 Main Street in Southbridge. Telephone 508-764-3341.

Golf
Heritage Country Club: off Route 20 in Charlton, 18 holes. Telephone 508-248-5111. Nichols College Golf Course: in Dudley, 18 holes. Telephone 508-943-9837.

Fishing in and
Around the Quabbin

Quabbin is known as an excellent cold-water fishery, with lake trout, land-locked salmon, and smallmouth bass the most sought-after fish. The MDC has established unique rules and regulations for the reservoir that differ from most bodies of water in Massachusetts. The fishing season at the Quabbin runs from mid-April to mid-October (call the MDC Visitor Center at 413-323-7221 for exact dates). Boats with six-to-nine-horsepower motors are available for rent at Gates 8, 31 and 43. If you bring your own boat, it must have a minimum length

Trout are stocked in the rivers and streams around Quabbin each spring.

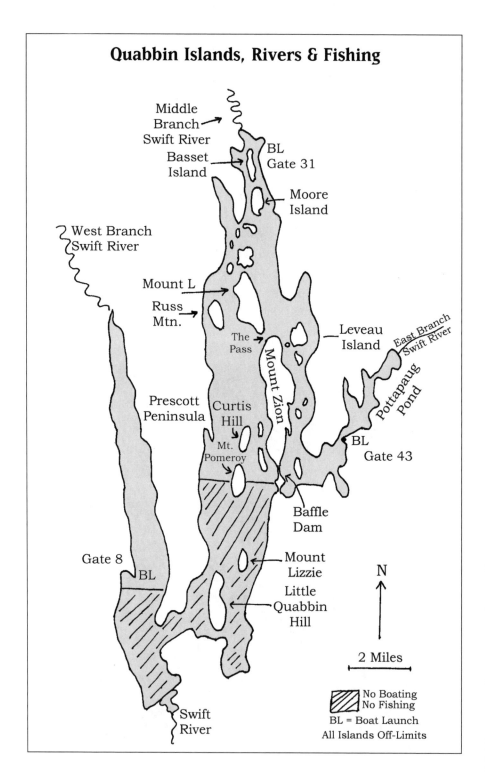

Quabbin Islands, Rivers & Fishing

Middle Branch Swift River

Basset Island

BL Gate 31

Moore Island

West Branch Swift River

Mount L

Russ Mtn.

The Pass

Leveau Island

East Branch Swift River

Prescott Peninsula

Curtis Hill

Mount Zion

Pottapaug Pond

Mt. Pomeroy

BL Gate 43

Baffle Dam

Gate 8

BL

Mount Lizzie

Little Quabbin Hill

N

2 Miles

No Boating
No Fishing

BL = Boat Launch

All Islands Off-Limits

Swift River

of twelve feet and the motor must be 20 horsepower or less. (Four-stroke engines are limited to an Outboard Council Rating of up to a maximum of 25 horsepower.) Shoreline fishing is allowed in all non-restricted areas during the regular Quabbin fishing season.

Canoeing is not allowed on the Quabbin Reservoir. Canoes can be launched on Pottapaug Pond at Gate 43 and above the regulating dam at Gate 31. Both of these areas are relatively shallow and have warmwater species. Canoes must be at least 12 feet in length. Carry-in boat access and use is allowed on South Spectacle and Bassett ponds. Boat fishing is allowed on Pepper's Mill Pond with non-motorized, carry-in boats.

You must have a Massachusetts fishing license to boat the Quabbin. A special one-day fishing license is now available at all three boat rental gates for people that only plan to visit the Quabbin once. Boat launching Area 1 at Gate 8 in Pelham is the prime area for coldwater species like trout and salmon. Boat launching Area 2 at Gate 31 in New Salem is known as a good bass area, in addition to trout and salmon. Boat launching Area 3 at Gate 43 in Hardwick also has a mix of warmwater and coldwater fish. Remember to steer clear of loons and bald eagles to avoid causing them stress. During nesting season the birds can easily be disturbed and may abandon their nests if approached too closely.

* * *

Joe Bergin, a fisheries biologist with the Massachusetts Division of Fisheries and Wildlife, oversees the fishery at the Quabbin, and he recently gave me a summary of how the different species were fairing.

The lake trout scenario is a mixture of good and bad news. "The good news," says Bergen, "is that the population is up and reproducing well. The bad news is that the lake trout are eating themselves out of house and home, and the number of large lake trout has been plummeting. To combat this problem we have established creel limits that put pressure on the smaller fish." For anglers this is a mixed blessing, but no matter what size of fish you are after, the best time to catch lakers is just after ice-out. In a normal year the fishing is the most productive in the early part of the season, and gets progressively more difficult as the lake trout head down to colder water in the depths of Quabbin. (There is also a token stocking of less than a hundred rainbow trout each year.)

Another prized game fish at the reservoir is the landlocked salmon, but it is not easily caught. Of the fisherman that exclusively angle for salmon, only one out of ten actually catch one. According to Bergin, "The low success rates of anglers are primarily due to the relatively low population of salmon. Quabbin is a low-fertility water and we supplement the wild spawning with yearly salmon smolts to keep the population steady." You can witness (but not fish for) migrating salmon during the fall when an annual "run" occurs in one of the Quabbin's tributaries during the November spawning period. Hop Brook, the West Branch of the Swift River and Underhill Brook get a limited run of salmon. The best time to see these runs occur on the day after a rainstorm, when the salmon are attracted to the stream's stronger flow.

You can increase your odds of catching a salmon during the spring and summer by understanding where the fish are located as the season progresses. Studies have shown that in the early spring, the salmon are found at a surface layer to a depth of ten feet, then gradually move to deeper water as the spring turns into summer. When the water temperature reaches its maximum of 52 to 54 degrees Farenheit the salmon are cruising 50 to 60 feet below the water surface.

Perhaps the biggest success story at the Quabbin is the smallmouth bass. Yearly catches are between 40,000 and 50,000, with one to two pounds being a typical weight. 90% of all fish are released by anglers. The peak fishing months are in May and June during the pre-spawn and spawning periods, when odds are good for catching one of the Quabbin's larger smallmouths in the four-pound range. (Largemouth bass are not nearly as numerous as smallmouths because the Quabbin is cold, deep and rocky— conditions which are more suited to smallmouth than largemouth bass. There are, however, a healthy population of white perch, with approximately 35,000 caught in a typical year.)

Nearby Rivers
Choosing a river to angle for trout in the greater Quabbin region is not an easy decision. There's a lot of productive water to explore (as well as a healthy population of blackflies in early May). All three branches of the Swift River that feed into the Quabbin have trout, and all are stocked. These rivers have both fast water and slow stretches with plenty of "pocket water" in between. Most of the trout I've caught in the branches have been rainbows. To see which roads cross the rivers, check out the maps in the Quick Guide section of this book. (The main branch of the Swift River which exits the Quabbin Reservoir is discussed at the end of this chapter.)

Other rivers of note include the Ware River, which is fairly slow flowing above Barre Plains. Faster water can be found downstream. Brook trout and browns are the two primary species stocked, and a few browns are said to hold over each year despite the fact that the water warms significantly in the summer. (On my "to-do" list is to take a canoe down the more isolated parts of the Ware River and stop at various sections to fish.) The upper branches of the river, called the east and west branches, run through Hubbardston and Rutland and also contain trout, although you may have to do a bit of bushwacking. Route 62 crosses the West Branch of the Ware River; and Brigham Road, a bumpy dirt road, crosses both branches. Hendrickson's and Blacknose Dace work well on all sections of the Ware River, and spin fisherman should try minnow-imitating lures.

The Quaboag River in Brookfield and Warren also deserves attention because it is one of the first rivers to warm up in the spring for fly fishing. It, too, is stocked, but this river can be difficult to wade during high-water. Try the section from the green bridge below West Warren downstream along Route 62 where there are a few runs of quickwater racing between boulders.

Along Route 2 in Wendell, Athol and Erving, the Millers River offers the angler stocked trout and smallmouth bass, along with a few holdover browns. A popular area is the Farley Flats stretch of boulders, rapids and pools located near the Farley Bridge, just west of the Erving Paper Mill. Wading is possible, but it is very slippery and felt soles are a must. If you want to explore back roads away from Route 2, try the upper branches of the Millers River in Royalston and South Royalston by Route 68, and north of Tullyville in Athol. Fly fishermen report that the river has abundant insect life.

For tips on the Swift River which exits the Quabbin, I've asked my friend Ed Hermenau to share his knowledge. Ed is one of those dedicated fly fishermen who has spent countless hours on the Swift, even a few in the dead of winter!

FISHING THE SWIFT RIVER
By Ed Hermenau
The first day I ever fished the Swift River I came prepared with the tiny flies I had heard I would need to catch the wary, educated fish of this catch-and-release tailwater. I was fishing close to the far bank in little pockets between clumps of alder bushes where I had seen a few subtle rises. Fishing a size 22 Griffith's Gnat on a 12 foot 6x leader, I was struggling to coordinate everything needed to get a

good drift. The wind, the trees behind me, the subtle currents in the flat water, and the small opening between the alders made getting a cast with a proper drift to the rising trout very difficult. I guess I was so satisfied with one of my few successful casts that I was not prepared when a trout actually took my fly. I did manage to set the hook and then hang on while the trout rocketed ten feet down stream. It leaped up—almost into an alder bush—then leaped back upstream to another other clump of alders, and then off of my line.

Thus I was introduced to the Swift River. The river has a very healthy population of rainbows, browns and brook trout which swim in the consistently cool waters that flow through the Winsor dam below the Quabbin Reservoir. Due to the catch-and-release regulations and the pressure that this river gets, these fish are easy to spook and at the same time very wary of anything but the best in presentation. They are clearly accustomed to having anglers in the water with them, and distinguishing between the real insects and our imitations.

I have found myself chuckling at a rising trout's willingness to inspect my offerings (without taking) only to look down and see a couple of decent-sized rainbows holding behind my legs. If you go to the Swift, I can almost guarantee that you will see very big trout cruising through crystal clear waters. You should also, however, be able to appreciate the irony of their refusal to cooperate with what you have on your mind. This is at the core of what makes fly fishing so interesting, entertaining, and, of course, frustrating. Something in the fish's make-up protects it from our intrusions. Unless everything—cast, drift, fly size and color—is like the real thing, the fish is not likely to strike. I have not been to a river where this is more readily observed than the Swift.

The Y-pool downstream of the dam release is home to a healthy population of very large and cautious trout. Standing at the edge of the drop-off, you can see them holding in the deep water or porpoising to take some natural fly at, or just below, the surface. Once put down by an angler, these fish seem to momentarily stop feeding and move down into the pool, only to resurface in another location and resume feeding.

These fish can be caught, but it is not easy. The traditional view is that tiny flies on long 6 and 7x tippets are necessary and this is true. Fishermen regularly hit the Swift armed with midge imitations, tiny mayflies and spinners in sizes 20-26, along with tiny nymphs fished just beneath the surface. However, taking a contrary tactic can also be successful. One day I watched a fisherman catch several 18 to 20-inch trout in the Y-pool using a fast sinking line and a crayfish pattern. My last fish at the Swift this past fall was caught on a size 10 bushy wet fly of unknown origin. (I'd found it in a fly box beside a road.) I had heard a splashy rise and decided the fish was after something substantial. I greased up the wet to float and cast over to where I had seen the rise, twitched the fly once, and he grabbed it. The fly looked more like a moth than anything else, but I had a very nice 14-inch rainbow.

The Swift can be divided into several sections with distinguishing characteristics. From the "bubbler" at the base of the dam down to the Y-pool, the river runs straight and swift over a bed of rocks and sand. This section is narrow and heavily shaded by pines, but look carefully and you will see many trout holding throughout. Try fishing this section with small beadhead nymphs, hare's ear nymphs, brassies or tiny drys but keep your movements slow and fish from the bank as much as possible. Where the run empties into the Y-pool the river separates into two riffles with some large rocks in the center. Then it widens out and gets much deeper, thus the name Y-pool. The temptation is to get right into the Y-pool itself but don't ignore riffles.

The Y-pool is the most popular section of the river to fish because of the size and number of fish holding in it. It is probably fifty yards long and forty to fifty feet wide. Be careful wading here. While you can easily see to the bottom, it is much deeper than it looks and there is a very steep drop-off. There are usually fishermen in the pool so take some time to observe what areas they are working before wading in. While anglers have to be willing to share this section due to the number who frequent it, there are still "zones" for each angler to work. Observe and respect the other angler's space and you will start to get a feel for what water you should be working.

Almost every time I have been to the Y-pool I have seen rising trout. On the surface use dark midges, spinners, Griffith's gnats, and emergers or nymphs in all in sizes 20-26. Don't be afraid to try something big (wooley buggers, crayfish) and go deep as well. I have also had luck using partridge and orange wets in sizes 16-20. In summer months I would try small terrestrials. Hoppers and crickets fished close to the rocky bank might produce some thrilling strikes under the right conditions.

After leaving the Y-pool the river runs for about a half-mile to the Route 9 bridge. This section is mostly slow-flowing flat water with some gentle bends and runs. Observe this water carefully, and you will see holding trout throughout and sporadic rises. Concentrate on deeper channels tight to the banks and deadfalls where the fish can remain hidden. I met a fisherman in this section one time having more success than anyone I had seen. He was using a size 20 nymph with a cream-colored body and redhead rigged with one split shot. While this section does not have the concentration of fish that the Y-pool does, there are fewer anglers and the odds of catching something are perhaps a bit better.

Just below the Route 9 bridge there is another very deep pool that always holds big fish. I have had the best success here using black CDC ants or cinnamon foam ants in sizes 16-18. The river downstream gets a little wilder and is clearly less fished than the upstream sections. Moving carefully and being observant, you will be able to spot and perhaps land some very large trout. (The river is actually canoeable near the middle of its length.)

One of my most memorable experiences at the Swift River came two years ago in early March. I had planned to go on Sunday, but the weather called for temperatures in the high 30's with rain, so I decided to go out on Saturday. I awoke to find light snow falling, but decided I'd rather fish in snow than rain, and made the two-hour drive, getting to the river at around 9am. Walking the path along the river, I could hear the faint hissing of the snow settling into the trees, along with the gentle sounds the river made as it flowed through white woods. After a few minutes of fishing, I felt the stresses of modern life vanish. I fished for about four hours that day, never saw another person or any sign of a trout, but it was one of the best days of fishing I ever experienced.

If you want to catch a great number of fish, do not come to the Swift River unless you are a true expert (even then my money would be on the fish). If, however, you want to have a shot at catching some very big fish that will test your skills, or if you simply get a kick out of observing trout that are completely in tune with their environment, come to the Swift. You won't be disappointed.

(As of this writing it is still uncertain what areas of the Swift River may be closed due to security. Obey all security related signs.)

Explorer's Information

LODGING

Amherst Motel (Amherst)
Host to the five-college area, one mile west on Route 9 from Amherst center.
(413-256-8122)
408 North Hampton Road (Route 9), Amherst, MA 01002

Antique 1880 Inn B&B (Ware)
Relax in yesterday charm: afternoon tea served by the fireplace and delicious breakfasts.
(413-967-7847)
14 Pleasant Street, Ware, MA 01082

Bullard Farm B&B and Conference Center (New Salem)
In addition to a traditional B&B, Bullard Farm also offers alternative arrangements for groups. Located one mile from Gate 29 at Quabbin Reservoir.
(978-544-6959)
89 Elm Street, New Salem, MA 01355

Comfort Inn & Suites Colonial (Sturbridge)
Three-story hotel surrounded by eight immaculately groomed acres overlooking Pistol Pond. The hotel features Colonial decor, indoor heated pool and whirlpool, outdoor pool, fitness room, lounge, complimentary continental breakfast, suites with fireplaces, Cracker Barrel Restaurant and Old Country Store on premises, and recipient of Choice Hotels International gold award designation.
(508-347-3306)
215 Charlton Road (PO Box 399), Sturbridge, MA 01566

Copper Lantern Motor Lodge (West Brookfield)

Sixteen regular rooms with refrigerator and microwaves, and eight efficiencies.
Room rates are from $48 to $62 per night.
(508-867-6441) (Fax 508-867-9635)
Route 9 (PO Box 1138)
West Brookfield, MA 01585

Elias Carter House on the Common (Brimfield)

Comfortable accommodations for a night or weekly.
Conveniently located on the Brimfield town common.
(413-245-3267)
8 North Main Street,
Brimfield, MA 01010

The Harding Allen Estate (Barre)

Magnificent mansion in pristine New England town. Visit them at
www.Harding-Allen.com
(978-355-4920)
Route 122, off Barre Common
PO Box 933
Barre, MA 01005

The Inn at Clamber Hill (Petersham)

Relax and refresh your spirits in the tranquility of a 33-acre "pre-Quabbin"
estate. Suites, double rooms, all private baths, eight fireplaces, two-course
gourmet breakfast included, library, wintergarden, garden, hiking paths-
"Peaceful Seclusion in a Grand Style."
(888-374-0007 or 978-724-8800) (www.clamberhill.com)
111 North Main Street,
Petersham, MA 01366

The Jenkins Inn and Restaurant (Barre)

Romantic lodging and fine dining at the heart of New England.
(800-378-7373)
7 West Street/Route 122 (PO Box 799),
Barre, MA 01005

Stevens Farm Bed & Breakfast (Barre)

A 350-acre nine generation farm with something for everyone: six guest rooms, inground pool, fishing, hiking, biking, skiing, small banquets and luncheons or meetings.

(978-355-2227) (stevensfarminn@juno.com)

749 Old Coldbrook Road,

Barre, MA 01005

Sturbridge Host Hotel (Sturbridge)

232 deluxe accommodations on Cedar Lake.

(508-347-7393)

366 Main Street

Sturbridge, MA 01566

The Wildwood Inn B & B (Ware)

The Wildwood Inn features 9 rooms, private baths, American primitive antiques, and early cradles and quilts. Two acres, wrap-around porch, gorgeous gardens and full country breakfast. ADA compliant and AAA rated.

(413-967-7798 and 800-860-8098)

121 Church Street

Ware, MA 01082

Winterwood at Petersham (Petersham)

Winterwood at Petersham is an 1842 historic Greek Revival mansion offering Bed and Breakfast and caters on-site private functions.

(978-724-8885) (www.winterwoodinn.com)

19 North Main Street,

Petersham, MA 01366

RESTAURANTS

The Historic Salem Cross Inn (West Brookfield)

Excellent food and drink are offered in the tradition of New England's generous hospitality. Built in 1705, the Salem Cross Inn is surrounded by wood and fieldstone fences and 600 acres of meadows and forest.

(508-867-8337)

Route 9,

West Brookfield, MA 01585

Sunburst Restaurant (Sturbridge)
Like your friend's kitchen. Open 7am - 2pm, Monday -Sunday, breakfast (all day) & lunch.
(508-347-3097)
Corner of Route 20 and Arnold Road (PO Box 555),
Sturbridge, MA 01566 White's Landing (see All Other)

FARMS/GARDENS/ORCHARDS

Brookfield Orchards (North Brookfield)
More than an apple orchard: apples, pastries, cider, snack bar, preserves, maple products, cheese, books, crafts, antiques and collectibles; truly unique!
(508-867-6858 or 1-877-622-7555)
12 Lincoln Road,
North Brookfield, MA 01535

Cook's Farm Orchard (Brimfield)
A retail/pick-your-own fruit farm featuring apple picking and homemade baked goods.
(413-245-3241)
106 Haynes Hill Road,
Brimfield, MA 01010

Hamilton Orchards (New Salem)
Pick-your-own fruit available from early July through late October; raspberries, blueberries, blackberries, and apples with the snack bar open on weekends.
(978-544-6867)
25 West Street,
New Salem, MA 01355

Red Apple Farm (Phillipston)
An old New England farm setting with a view from the high orchards. Apples, peaches, pears, blueberries, raspberries and pumpkins available, or pick-your-own. Plus apple pie and dumplings. Farm animals, hayrides, and weekend BBQ's.
(978-249-6763 or 800-628-4851)
455 Highland Avenue,
Phillipston, MA 01331

ANTIQUES/ARTS/CRAFTS

Blue Cupboard Gift Shop (North Brookfield)
Located in an early 1800's farmhouse. Artist in residence creates own hand-decorated pottery and handcrafted tin ware. Hours are 11am-5pm Wednesday-Saturday, 1pm-5pm on Sundays.
(508-867-9869)
24 Bates Street,
North Brookfield, MA 01535

Diamond T Gallery (Baldwinville)
Offering art of all subject matter and medium including LTD, originals, posters, canvas transfers, sculptures, custom matting, framing and specialty shop with Native-American jewelry and crafts. The largest art gallery west of Boston, just off Route 2.
(978-939-4282) (www.diamondtgallery.com)
74 Maple Street,
Baldwinville, MA 01436

Les Campbell's Sky Meadow Studio & Photo Gallery (Belchertown)
Les Campbell is an award-winning photographer known for both the diversity of his photography and for his stunning images of the Quabbin. See the write-up about Les at the back of this book.
(413-323-7405)
Route 9,
Belchertown, MA 01007

Petersham Crafts Center (Petersham)
Arts, crafts, books and more! Located just north of the Petersham common on Route 32. Open Wednesdays through Sundays, 12pm to 4pm.
(978-724-3415)
PO Box 235
Petersham, MA 02056

The Quilt and Cabbage (Sturbridge)
An avid quilter's haven of fabrics, books, stencils, notions, etc.
(508-347-3023)
538 Main Street (PO Box 534)
Sturbridge, MA 01566 White's Landing (see All Other)

MUSEUMS

The Stone House Museum (Belchertown)
Built in 1827 as a wedding present, this stately 10 room Federal Style home maintains an impressive collection of American furniture, china, and decorative accessories. The museum also offers a working turn-of-the-century print shop and the Ford Annex which houses the museum's carriages, sleighs and stage coach.

Open mid-may through October on Wednesdays and Saturdays from 2 to 5pm, and year-round by appointment.

(413-323-6573)

20 Maple Street, Route 202

Belchertown, MA 01007

ALL OTHER

In Balance - A Massage Therapy Center for the Whole Family (E. Brookfield)
In Balance offers Swedish, relaxation and therapeutic massage; pregnancy, post partum and infant massage, craniosacral and myofascial therapy for children and adults. Also offers sports, deep tissue and hot stone massage, reiki and health workshops.

(508-867-2700)

Martha Davis, LMT, owner

394 East Main Street

East Brookfield, MA 01515

North Quabbin Woods
Visit the North Quabbin Woods website at www.northquabbinwoods.org for all kinds of forest related information about the North Quabbin area including ecotourism, locally made wood products, maps and more! North Quabbin Woods is a project of the New England Forestry Foundation.

PO Box 27, 450 West River Street

Orange, MA 01364

Tri-Community Area Chamber of Commerce (Sturbridge)
Call or stop in for traveler's information for greater Sturbridge.

(508-347-2761)

380 Main Street (Route 20)

Sturbridge, MA 01566

White's Landing (Brookfield)

Canoe rentals, river cruises, hot dog stand/coffee shop, ice cream, bait and tackle, local and historical information.
(508-867-5561)
Route 148 (7 Fiskdale Road)
Brookfield, MA 01560

W.H. King Realty & Appraisal (West Brookfield)

Real estate consultation and buyer agency services to maximize your objectives.
(508-867-2600)
147 West Main Street (PO Box 585),
West Brookfield, MA 01585-0585

FAVORITE COUNTRY STORES

The Country Store (On the common in Petersham)

A 160 year old country store in the heart of a beautiful New England community, surrounded by protected lands. Full groceries and gifts. Homemade good for lunch daily.

The Hardwick Store (On the common in Hardwick)

Small country store/deli. Homemade baked goods, soups and salads. Sandwiches made to order with Boar's Head Brand meats and cheeses. Take out/eat in.

New Salem General Store (Route 202, New Salem)

A full service country store in beautiful New Salem.

Reed's Country Store (Barre Road/Route 67, New Braintree)

A handsome, old fashioned country store.

Final Thoughts

Les Campbell helped me launch this project several years ago when I spent a few hours at his house at Sky Meadow Farm near the Quabbin. I told him about my idea for a book about the Quabbin, combining history with an explorer's guide, and Les warmed to the idea immediately, giving me full access to his many historical photographs and documents. We had never met before this visit, but because of our mutually strong feelings for the Quabbin, we hit it off, and I must have asked Les a hundred questions about the reservoir. He graciously answered every one, but it was an unsolicited comment that really helped me. "Mike," Les said, "many writers have tried to tackle Quabbin and do a new book on it, but after they get started they become overwhelmed and give up."

Within weeks I knew what he meant. The Quabbin was like opening up a door which led to two more doors, which led to four more doors, and so on. There were just so many different aspects a writer could cover; it would be easy to drown in your own research. As I kept opening those doors, I did become overwhelmed; but I'd hear Les' words, almost as a challenge, and become focused again. Eventually I came to understand that the best way for me to approach this was not to try and cover every little bit of history, but rather give the reader an overview with anecdotes from the people who were there when the valley was taken. I felt that if I could open those first few doors for readers, they would become as curious as I was and want to experience the magic of the Quabbin themselves. That is why this book is filled with maps, directions, and suggestions.

While the writing was a challenge, the research for this book was full of fun. On each weekend trip I'd see something new, learn a bit of overlooked history, or meet a unique individual. There was that special day with Earl Cooley, sitting in the cave he called the Indian Kitchen, talking about days gone by and looking out at the rain. There were the many trips I spent looking for the headstone with the poison oyster, only to eventually find out from Robert Keyes that the headstone had an inscription about a poison oyster, not an actual carving of one. No wonder I couldn't find it!

On one of those hunts for this strange headstone, an odd thing happened to me. I was wandering around a graveyard set back off a dirt road, discouraged that I still hadn't located it, when I met a woman out walking her dog. I asked her if she knew of the headstone, and she said she'd heard of it but didn't know which cemetery it was in. I thanked her and as I was about to leave, she said, "You wouldn't happen to be that writer, Michael Tougias, would you?" My jaw dropped. Never have I been recognized anywhere before. "How did you recognize me?" I asked. "I didn't," she replied, "I just knew you were the kind of guy that liked these back roads and forgotten places."

Two years later I was showing some friends the hollow tree at Dana center, when another hiker wandered over. He asked, "Are you Michael Tougias?" Again I asked how he knew. He answered, "I just guessed. I read your columns [*The Union News,* Springfield, MA] and I thought who else would be showing people a hollow tree." On another trip I met a hiker and he recommended I visit the Bear's Den. After I told him I'd been there many times, he said, "Have you ever seen the bowl-shaped depression in the granite cliff overlooking the waterfall?" I'd never even heard of it let alone seen it, so off I went, scrambling up the cliffs at the Bears Den, excited to find yet another surprise. What I learned from these encounters, and several others, was there were many other kindred spirits who enjoyed roaming around greater Quabbin, seeking out hidden places and solitude.

The Quabbin means many things to different people, and to many it's a refuge not only for wildlife but also for individuals in search of solitude. In a way, these benefits are the silver lining to the destruction of the lost towns. If I was going to lose my home and be forced to move, at least I'd be consoled if I knew that natural beauty would replace my loss.

Lois Barnes, one of the former residents of two of the lost towns, summed it up best when she said, "If the towns were still there they might be full of McDonald's and other development. At least we have memories of the towns the way they were." And Les Campbell puts it another way: "If we hadn't sent Boston water from the valley, Boston might have moved out here. I'd much rather send them the water."

About the Author

Michael Tougias is the author of several books about New England, gives frequent slide presentations, and leads spring and fall tours of the Quabbin Reservoir. He spends much of his free time relaxing in Northern Vermont at his rustic cabin, which is the subject of his next book, *There's a Porcupine in My Outhouse!* (September 2002 release). He also volunteers leading visually impaired people on nature walks and lends his efforts to protecting open spaces.

Ordering Books

To order autographed copies of Tougias' books send a check to him at PO Box 72, Norfolk, MA 02056 and include $2 per book for shipping. His books are as follows:

- River Days: Exploring the Connecticut River from Source to Sea ($14.95)
- King Philip's War: The History and Legacy of America's Forgotten Conflict (co-author with Eric Schultz) ($18.95)
- Until I Have No Country (A novel of King Philip's War) ($14.95)
- New England Wild Places ($12.95)
- Autumn Rambles of New England (co-author Mark Tougias) ($14.95)
- Quiet Places of Massachusetts ($13.95)
- Nature Walks in Eastern Massachusetts ($12.95)
- More Nature Walks in Eastern Massachusetts ($12.95)
- Nature Walks in Central and Western Massachusetts (with R. Laubach) ($12.95)
- Country Roads of Massachusetts ($13.95)
- Exploring The Hidden Charles ($12.95)
- A Taunton River Journey ($10.95)
- There's a Porcupine in My Outhouse! ($18.95)

Slide Presentations

Tougias offers slide presentations on the topics in each of his books, including the Quabbin. You can have your local library or club contact him at PO Box 72, Norfolk, MA 02056 to schedule a presentation.

Tours and Workshops

To inquire about the next tours to the Quabbin Reservoir led by Tougias, contact the Keefe Technical School for Continuing Education in Framingham, the Stony Brook Wildlife Sanctuary in Norfolk, or the Boston Learning Society in Needham.

For information on the author's next "Get Published" workshop, write to Michael Tougias at PO Box 72, Norfolk, MA 02056.

You can also visit Tougias' website at www.michaeltougias.com.

Les Campbell

Les Campbell has captured the spirit of Quabbin in a wide array of stunning photographs. He has lived by the Quabbin since its creation and has worked there for 44 years in the MDC's Water Quality Laboratory, and in 1984 helped establish the Quabbin Visitor Center.

By making new and permanent negatives from old photographs and sharing them with the public, Les has preserved the visual history of the Quabbin. Through his own photography Les reflects the essence of the Quabbin, capturing the reservoir and the surrounding forests in all seasons and in all moods, from mist rising from the water on a summer's morning to waves pounding the shore during a winter storm.

At his gallery at his "Sky Meadow" homestead in Belchertown, Les displays his photographs in order to share his vision and respect for the Quabbin. His gallery is open on Wednesdays from June through October (2-4p.m.) and on Sundays in April, May, November and December (2-4pm) or by appointment (telephone 413-323-7405). Groups can also contact Les for the variety of slide presentations he offers at his gallery. The gallery is located at the end of a dirt road on the south side of Route 9, one-half mile east of the west entrance to Quabbin Park, or 500 feet west of the Belchertown/Ware town line.

Recommended Reading
and Primary Sources

Most of my research material was made available through the courtesy of the Metropolitan District Commission, the Friends of the Quabbin and the Swift River Valley Historical Society. I also gained valuable information from the many people I interviewed who grew up in the lost towns, people whose parents were involved in the construction of the Quabbin, and those involved in its administration and operation. Most of those knowledgeable people are listed in the acknowledgements.

I recommend the following books and booklets for those who would like to further their education on all aspects of the Quabbin. Additional information can be found at the headquarters of the organizations listed above as well as the public libraries of towns near the Quabbin, especially Amherst.

Barnes, Lois and Yeisley, Lisa. *Here Was Home* (Audio Tape). Belchertown, MA. Friends of Quabbin/MDC. 1995.

Christenson, James. "Real Estate Acquisitions for the Metropolitan Boston's Water Supply." *Journal of the New England Water Works Association,* Volume 59. 1945.

Conuel, Thomas. *Quabbin: The Accidental Wilderness.* Lincoln, Massachusetts. The Massachusetts Audubon Society. 1981.

Friends of Quabbin, Inc./MDC. *Quabbin Facts and Figures.* Belchertown, MA. 1996.

Friends of Quabbin, Inc./MDC. *Letters From Quabbin* (Republished articles from the Springfield Union.) Belchertown, MA. 1996.

Greene, J.R. *The Creation of Quabbin Reservoir.* Athol, MA. The Transcript Press. 1981.

Greene, J.R. *Historic Quabbin Hikes*. Athol, MA. Highland Press. 1994.

Gustafson, Evelina. *Ghost Towns 'Neath Quabbin Reservoir*. Boston, MA. Amity Press. 1940.

Howe, Donald. *Quabbin, the Lost Valley*. Ware, MA. The Quabbin Book House. 1951.

Navas, Deborah. *Murdered by His Wife*. Amherst, MA. University of Massachusetts Press. 2001.

Russell, J.W. *Vestiges of the Lost Valley: Buildings and Bells from Quabbin*. 1986.

Schultz, Eric and Tougias, Michael. *King Philip's War*. Woodstock, VT. Countryman Press. 1998.

Wilkie, Richard and Tager, Jack. *Historical Atlas of Massachusetts*. Amherst, MA. The University of Massachusetts Press, 1991.

Yolen, Jane. *Letting Swift River Go* (for children). Boston, MA. Little, Brown and Company. 1992.

Index

INDEX

Other Books from On Cape Publications

The Blizzard of '78 by Michael Tougias

Windmills of New England by Daniel Lombardo

Haunted Inns of New England by Mark Jasper

The Boston Dictionary by John Powers

The Boston Handbook by John Powers

In The Footsteps of Thoreau: 25 Historic & Nature Walks on Cape Cod by Adam Gamble

A Guide to Nature on Cape Cod & the Islands edited by Greg O'Brien

Cape Cod, Martha's Vineyard & Nantucket, the Geologic Story by Robert Oldale

Walking the Shores of Cape Cod by Elliott Carr

Sea Stories of Cape Cod & the Islands by Admont Clark

Baseball by the Beach: A History of America's National Pastime on Cape Cod by Christopher Price

Cape Cod Confidential: True Tales of Murder, Crime & Scandal from the Pilgrims to the Present by Evan J. Albright

Haunted Cape Cod & the Islands by Mark Jasper

www.oncapepublications.com